Stories from Asia

**A collection of short stories from South Asia:
India, Pakistan and Bangladesh**

Selected and edited by
Madhu Bhinda

For Bhabi and Dhirubhai

Acknowledgements

Thanks are due to the many students with whom I
tried and tested stories included in this collection: their
involved oral and written responses provided valuable
feedback both for the selection of stories as well as in
planning the classroom activities.

Contents

Charity

To the Student

Whatever our cultural background, we all tell stories: they help us to make sense of our world and to see how we – as females or as males – may play our part in it. The views of the world created by the writers in this book show us the enormously rich variety of ways in which we all think, feel and behave in our different cultural groups. In doing so, the stories also help us to learn the value of sympathy, and of how much we really have in common with those who appear to be different from us.

To make sure that the stories included in this book are fun to read and stimulating to talk about, I have tried many of them with my own students. I am grateful to them for their enthusiastic responses, and would like to think that you too will share their pleasure.

There are sixteen in total – eight by women writers and eight by male writers. All of them deal with situations which may be familiar as well as unfamiliar to you, but in a way which touches our own lives in one way or another: they make us look at people, their relationships and their situations in a fresh and deeper way; in the process we learn something about ourselves, the society in which we live, as well as the different societies in which the characters themselves live.

You will notice from the Contents list that stories which are linked in various ways have been placed in groups of two or three. Your reading of any one story may well be altered and enriched by your reading of the other(s) in a group. To help you with your work, I have offered many activities at the back of this book. These provide ideas for group discussion of individual stories, for exploring similarities and differences between linked stories, and for writing. You will find lots of choice, and you may write imaginatively in response to a story, or discuss the stories themselves in a critical way. All these activities are designed to meet your examination coursework needs. The section entitled 'Compare and Contrast Stories' (page 187) is intended to help you with writing an extended essay on those story combinations that may have especially appealed to you.

Madhu Bhinda

India, Pakistan and Bangladesh

Anita Desai

A Devoted Son

When the results appeared in the morning papers, Rakesh scanned them, barefoot and in his pyjamas at the garden gate, then went up the steps to the veranda where his father sat sipping his morning tea and bowed down to touch his feet.

'A first division, son?' his father asked, beaming, reaching for the papers.

'At the top of the list, Papa,' Rakesh murmured, as if awed. 'First in the country.'

Bedlam broke loose then. The family whooped and danced. The whole day long visitors streamed into the small yellow house at the end of the road, to congratulate the parents of this Wunderkind, to slap Rakesh on the back and fill the house and garden with the sounds and colours of a festival. There were garlands and *halwa*[1], party clothes and gifts (enough fountain pens to last years, even a watch or two), nerves and temper and joy, all in a multicoloured whirl of pride and great shining vistas newly opened: Rakesh was the first son in the family to receive an education, so much had been sacrified in order to send him to school and then medical college, and at last the fruits of their sacrifice had arrived, golden and glorious.

To everyone who came to him to say, 'Mubarak, Varmaji, your son has brought you glory', the father

[1] sweets

5

said, 'Yes, and do you know what is the first thing he did when he saw the results this morning? He came and touched my feet. He bowed down and touched my feet.' This moved many of the women in the crowd so much that they were seen to raise the ends of their saris and dab at their tears while the men reached out for the betel leaves and sweetmeat that were offered around on trays and shook their heads in wonder and approval of such exemplary filial behaviour. 'One does not often see such behaviour in sons any more,' they all agreed, a little enviously perhaps. Leaving the house, some of the women said, sniffing, 'At least on such an occasion they might have served pure ghee sweets,' and some of the men said, 'Don't you think old Varma was giving himself airs? He needn't think we don't remember that he came from the vegetable market himself, his father used to sell vegetables, and he has never seen the inside of a school.' But there was more envy than rancour in their voices and it was, of course, inevitable – not every son in that shabby little colony at the edge of the city was destined to shine as Rakesh shone, and who knew that better than the parents themselves?

And that was only the beginning, the first step in a great, sweeping ascent to the radiant heights of fame and fortune. The thesis he wrote for his MD brought Rakesh still greater glory, if only in select medical circles. He won a scholarship. He went to the USA (that was what his father learnt to call it and taught the whole family to say – not America, which was what the ignorant neighbours called it, but, with a grand familiarity, 'the USA') where he pursued his career in the most prestigious of all hospitals and won encomiums from his American colleagues which were relayed to his admiring and glowing family. What was more, he came back, he actually returned to that small yellow house in the once-new but increasingly shabby colony, right at the end of the road where the rubbish vans tipped out their stinking contents for pigs to nose in and rag-pickers to build their shacks on, all steaming and smoking just outside the neat wire fences and well-tended gardens. To this Rakesh returned and the first thing he did on entering the house was to slip out of the embraces of his sisters and brothers and bow down and touch his father's feet.

As for his mother, she gloated chiefly over the strange fact that he had not married in America, had not brought home a foreign wife as all her neighbours had warned her he would, for wasn't that what all Indian boys went abroad for? Instead he agreed, almost without argument, to marry a girl she had picked out for him in her own village, the daughter of a childhood friend, a plump and uneducated girl, it was true, but so old-fashioned, so placid, so complaisant that she slipped into the household and settled in like a charm, seemingly too lazy and too good-natured to even try and make Rakesh leave home and set up independently, as any other girl might have done. What was more, she was pretty – really pretty, in a plump, pudding way that only gave way to fat – soft, spreading fat, like warm wax – after the birth of their first baby, a son, and then what did it matter?

For some years Rakesh worked in the city hospital, quickly rising to the top of the administrative organisa-tion, and was made a director before he left to set up his own clinic. He took his parents in his car – a new, sky-blue Ambassador with a rear window full of stickers and charms revolving on strings – to see the clinic when it was built, and the large sign-board over the door on which his name was printed in letters of red, with a row of degrees and qualifications to follow it like so many little black slaves of the regent. Thereafter his fame seemed to grow just a little dimmer – or maybe it was only that everyone in town had grown accustomed to it at last – but it was also the beginning of his fortune for he now became known not only as the best but also the richest doctor in town.

However, all this was not accomplished in the wink of an eye. Naturally not. It was the achievement of a lifetime and it took up Rakesh's whole life. At the time he set up his clinic his father had grown into an old man and retired from his post at the kerosene dealer's depot at which he had worked for forty years, and his mother died soon after, giving up the ghost with a sigh that sounded positively happy, for it was her own son who ministered to her in her last illness and who sat pressing her feet at the last moment – such a son as few women had borne.

For it had to be admitted – and the most unsuccessful and most rancorous of neighbours eventually did so – that Rakesh was not only a devoted son and a miraculously good natured man who contrived somehow to obey his parents and humour his wife and show concern equally for his children and his patients, but there was actually a brain inside this beautifully polished and formed body of good manners and kind nature and, in between ministering to his family and playing host to many friends and coaxing them all into feeling happy and grateful and content, he had actually trained his hands as well and emerged an excellent doctor, a really fine surgeon. How one man – and a man born to illiterate parents, his father having worked for a kerosene dealer and his mother having spent her life in a kitchen – had achieved, combined and conducted such a medley of virtues, no one could fathom, but all acknowledged his talent and skill.

It was a strange fact, however, that talent and skill, if displayed for too long, cease to dazzle. It came to pass that the most admiring of all eyes eventually faded and no longer blinked at his glory. Having retired from work and having lost his wife, the old father vey quickly went to pieces, as they say. He developed so many complaints and fell ill so frequently and with such mysterious diseases that even his son could no longer make out when it was something of significance and when it was merely a peevish whim. He sat huddled on his string bed most of the day and developed an exasperating habit of stretching out suddenly and lying absolutely still, allowing the whole family to fly around him in a flap, wailing and weeping, and then suddenly sitting up, stiff and gaunt, and spitting out a big gob of betel juice as if to mock their behaviour.

He did this once too often: there had been a big party in the house, a birthday party for the youngest son, and the celebrations had to be suddenly hushed, covered up and hustled out of the way when the daughter-in-law discovered, or thought she discovered, that the old man, stretched out from end to end of his string bed, had lost his pulse; the party broke up, dissolved, even turned into a band of mourners, when the old man sat up and the distraught daughter-in-law received a gob of red spittle right on the hem of her new organza sari. After that no one much cared if he sat up cross-legged on his bed, hawking and spitting, or lay down flat and turned grey as a corpse. Except, of course, for that pearl amongst pearls, his son Rakesh.

It was Rakesh who brought him his morning tea not in one of the china cups from which the rest of the family drank, but in the old man's favourite brass tumbler, and sat at the edge of his bed, comfortable and relaxed with the string of his pyjamas dangling out from under his fine lawn night-shirt, and discussed or, rather, read out the morning news to his father. It made no difference to him that his father made no response apart from spitting. It was Rakesh, too, who, on returning from the clinic in the evening, persuaded the old man to come out of his room, as bare and desolate as a cell, and take the evening air out in the garden, beautifully arranging the pillows and bolsters on the divan in the corner of the open veranda. On summer nights he saw to it that the servants carried out the old man's bed onto the lawn and himself helped his father down the steps and onto the bed, soothing him and settling him down for a night under the stars.

All this was very gratifying for the old man. What was not so gratifying was that he even undertook to supervise his father's diet. One day when the father was really sick, having ordered his daughter-in-law to make him a dish of *sooji halwa* and eaten it with a saucerful of cream, Rakesh marched into the room, not with his usual respectful step but with the confident and rather contemptuous stride of the famous doctor, and declared, 'No more halwa for you, Papa. We must be sensible, at your age. If you must have something sweet, Veena will cook you a little *kheer*, that's light, just a little rice and milk. But nothing fried, nothing rich. We can't have this happening again.'

The old man who had been lying stretched out on his bed, weak and feeble after a day's illness, gave a start at the very sound, the tone of these words. He opened his eyes – rather, they fell open with shock – and he stared at his son with disbelief that darkened quickly to reproach. A son who actually refused his father the food he craved? No, it was unheard of, it was incredible. But Rakesh had turned his back to him and was cleaning up the litter of bottles and packets on the medicine shelf and did not notice while Veena slipped silently out of the room with a little smirk that only the old man saw, and hated.

Halwa was only the first item to be crossed off the old man's diet. One delicacy after the other went — everything fried to begin with, then everything sweet, and eventually everything, everything that the old man enjoyed. The meals that arrived for him on the shining stainless steel tray twice a day were frugal to say the least – dry bread, boiled lentils, boiled vegetables and, if there was a bit of chicken or fish, that was boiled too. If he called for another helping – in a cracked voice that quavered theatrically – Rakesh himself would come to the door, gaze at him sadly and shake his head, saying, 'Now, Papa, we must be careful, we can't risk another illness, you know,' and although the daughter-in-law kept tactfully out of the way, the old man could just see her smirk sliding merrily through the air. He tried to bribe his grandchildren into buying him sweets (and how he missed his wife now, that generous, indulgent and illiterate cook), whispering, 'Here's fifty *paise*' as he stuffed the coins into a tight, hot fist. 'Run down to the shop at the crossroads and buy me thirty paise worth of *jalebis*[2] and you can spend the remaining twenty paise on yourself. Eh? Understand? Will you do that?' He got away with it once or twice but then was found out, the conspirator was scolded by his father and smacked by his mother and Rakesh came storming into the room, almost tearing his hair as he shouted through compressed lips, 'Now Papa, are you trying to turn my little son into a liar? Quite apart from spoiling your own stomach, you are spoiling him as well – you are encouraging him to lie to his own parents. You should have heard the lies

[2] flour spirals in syrup

he told his mother when she saw him bringing back those jalebis wrapped up in a filthy newspaper. I don't allow anyone in my house to buy sweets in the bazaar, Papa, surely you know that. There's cholera in the city, typhoid, gastroenteritis – I see these cases daily in the hospital, how can I allow my own family to run such risks?' The old man sighed and lay down in the corpse position. But that worried no one any longer.

There was only one pleasure left the old man now (his son's early morning visits and readings from the newspaper could no longer be called that) and those were visits from elderly neighbours. These were not frequent as his contemporaries were mostly as decrepit and helpless as he and few could walk the length of the road to visit him any more. Old Bhatia, next door, however, who was still spry enough to refuse, adamantly, to bathe in the tiled bathroom indoors and to insist on carrying out his brass mug and towel, in all seasons and usually at impossible hours, into the yard and bathe noisily under the garden tap, would look over the hedge to see if Varma were out on his veranda and would call to him and talk while he wrapped his *dhoti*[3] about him and dried the sparse hair on his head, shivering with enjoyable exaggeration. Of course these conversations, bawled across the hedge by two rather deaf old men conscious of having their entire households overhearing them, were not very satisfactory but Bhatia occasionally came out of his yard, walked down the bit of road and came in at Varma's gate to collapse onto the stone plinth built under the temple tree. If Rakesh were at home he would help his father down the steps into the garden and arrange him on his night bed under the tree and leave the two old men to chew betel leaves

[3] a long piece of cloth worn round the waist by Hindu men and boys

and discuss the ills of their individual bodies with combined passion.

'At least you have a doctor in the house to look after you,' sighed Bhatia, having vividly described his martyrdom to piles.

'Look after me?' cried Varma, his voice cracking like an ancient clay jar. 'He – he does not even give me enough to eat.'

'What? said Bhatia, the white hairs in his ears twitching. 'Doesn't give you enough to eat? Your own son?'

'My own son. If I ask him for one more piece of bread, he says no, Papa, I weighed out the *ata*[4] myself and I can't allow you to have more that two hundred grammes of cereal a day. He weighs the food he gives me, Bhatia – he has scales to weigh it on. That is what it has come to.'

'Never,' murmured Bhatia in disbelief. 'Is it possible, even in the evil age, for a son to refuse his father food?'

'Let me tell you,' Varma whispered eagerly. 'Today the family was having fried fish – I could smell it. I called to my daughter-in-law to bring me a piece. She came to the door and said No . . .'

'Said No?' It was Bhatia's voice that cracked. A drongo shot out of the tree and sped away. 'No?'

'No, she said no, Rakesh has ordered her to give me nothing fried. No butter, he says, no oil –'

'No butter? No oil? How does he expect his father to live?'

Old Varma nodded with melancholy triumph. 'That is how he treats me – after I have brought him up, given him an education, made him a great doctor. Great doctor! This is the way great doctors treat their

[4] flour

fathers, Bhatia,' for the son's sterling personality and character now underwent a curious sea change. Outwardly all might be the same but the interpretation had altered: his masterly efficiency was nothing but cold heartlessness, his authority was only tyranny in disguise.

There was cold comfort in complaining to neighbours and, on such a miserable diet, Varma found himself slipping, weakening and soon becoming a genuinely sick man. Powders and pills and mixtures were not only brought in when dealing with a crisis like an upset stomach but became a regular part of his diet – became his diet, complained Varma, supplanting the natural foods he craved. There were pills to regulate his bowel movements, pills to bring down his blood pressure, pills to deal with his arthritis, and, eventually, pills to keep his heart beating. In between there were panicky rushes to the hospital, some humiliating experiences with the stomach pump and enema, which left him frightened and helpless. He cried easily, shrivelling up on his bed, but if he complained of a pain or even a vague, grey fear in the night, Rakesh would simply open another bottle of pills and force him to take one. 'I have my duty to you, Papa,' he said when his father begged to be let off.

'Let me be,' Varma begged, turning his face away from the pill on the outstretched hand, 'Let me die. It would be better. I do not want to live only to eat your medicines.'

'Papa, be reasonable.'

'I leave that to you,' the father cried with sudden spirit. 'Let me alone, let me die now, I cannot live like this.'

'Lying all day on his pillows, fed every few hours by his daughter-in-law's own hands, visited by every member of his family daily – and then he says he does not want to live "like this",' Rakesh was heard to say, laughing, to someone outside the door.

'Deprived of food,' screamed the old man on the bed, 'his wishes ignored, taunted by his daughter-in-law, laughed at by his grandchildren – that is how I live.' But he was very old and weak and all anyone heard was an incoherent croak, some expressive grunts and cries of genuine pain. Only once, when old Bhatia had come to see him and they sat together under the temple tree, they heard his cry, 'God is calling me – and they won't let me go.'

The quantities of vitamins and tonics he was made to take were not altogether useless. They kept him alive and even gave him a kind of strength that made him hang on long after he ceased to wish to hang on. It was as though he were straining at a rope, trying to break it, and it would not break, it was still strong. He only hurt himself, trying.

In the evening, that summer, the servants would come into his cell, grip his bed, one at each end, and carry it out to the veranda, there setting it down with a thump that jarred every tooth in his head. In answer to his agonised complaints they said the Doctor Sahib had told them he must take the evening air and the evening air they would make him take – thump. Then Veena, that smiling, hypocritical pudding in a rustling sari, would appear and pile up the pillows under his head till he was propped up stiffly into a sitting position that made his head swim and his back ache. 'Let me lie down,' he begged, 'I can't sit up any more.'

'Try, Papa, Rakesh said you can if you try,' she said, and drifted away to the other end of the veranda where her transistor radio vibrated to the lovesick tunes from the cinema that she listened to all day.

So there he sat, like some still corpse, terrified, gazing out on the lawn where his grandsons played cricket, in danger of getting one of their hard spun balls in his eye, and at the gate that opened on to the dusty and rubbish-heaped lane but still bore, proudly, a newly touched-up signboard that bore his son's name and qualifications, his own name having vanished from the gate long ago.

At last the sky-blue Ambassador arrived, the cricket game broke up in haste, the car drove in smartly and the doctor, the great doctor, all in white, stepped out. Someone ran up to take his bag from him, others to escort him up the steps. 'Will you have tea?' his wife called, turning down the transistor set, 'or a Coca-Cola? Shall I fry you some samosas?' But he did not reply or even glance in her direction. Ever a devoted son, he went first to the corner where his father sat gazing, stricken, at some undefined spot in the dusty yellow air that swam before him. He did not turn his head to look at his son. But he stopped gobbling air with his uncontrolled lips and set his jaw as hard as a sick and very old man could set it.

'Papa,' his son said, tenderly, sitting down on the edge of the bed and reaching out to press his feet.

Old Varma tucked his feet under him, out of the way, and continued to gaze stubbornly into the yellow air of the summer evening.

'Papa, I'm home.'

Varma's hand jerked suddenly, in a sharp, decisive movement, but he did not speak.

'How are you feeling, Papa?'

Then Varma turned and looked at his son. His face was so out of control and all in pieces, that the multitude of expressions that crossed it could not make up a whole and convey to the famous man exactly what his father thought of him, his skill, his art.

'I'm dying,' he croaked. 'Let me die, I tell you.'

'Papa, you're joking,' his son smiled at him, lovingly. 'I've brought you a new tonic to make you feel better. You must take it, it will make you feel stronger again. Here it is. Promise me you will take it regularly, Papa.'

Varma's mouth worked as hard as though he still had a gob of betel in it (his supply of betel had been cut off years ago). Then he spat out some words, as sharp and bitter as poison, into his son's face. 'Keep your tonic – I want none – I want none – I won't take any more of – of your medicines. None. Never,' and he swept the bottle out of his son's hand with a wave of his own, suddenly grand, suddenly effective.

His son jumped, for the bottle was smashed and thick brown syrup had splashed up, staining his white trousers. His wife let out a cry and came running. All around the old man was hubbub once again, noise, attention.

He gave one push to the pillows at his back and dislodged them so he could sink down on his back, quite flat again. He closed his eyes and pointed his chin at the ceiling, like some dire prophet, groaning, 'God is calling me – now let me go.'

Ila Arab Mehta

Smoke

Translated from the Gujarati

Ba[1] comes back this evening by the five o'clock train.
Shubha glanced at her watch. It was only four o'clock,
still some time to go. A vast sea of overpowering emptiness engulfed her being. Nothing left to do.
Nothing . . . except wait.

Her hands wandered over the books lying on the
table and picked one up. It was a fat book written in
English, on women's health problems and their treatment. It opened with the picture of a naked woman,
bared in vivid detail, sketched with dexterity. For
clinical purposes only, of course!

She slammed it shut, pushed it back and walked
out of the room on to the open balcony. She stood
still. The oppressive tormenting afternoon was still
astride the earth, its heat permeating every nook and
cranny. 'Like my own emptiness,' she thought. 'Not a
hollow neutral vacuum but this leaden emptiness,
opaque and solid.

'The russet evening shall wax but a few moments
only. And then all will be dark again.' A wan smile on
her lips, Shubha stepped back into the room.

Just half-past four. Driving her car towards the
station, Dr Shubha scolded herself, 'You're becoming
neurotic, Shubha. The sun itself looks like a dark blot to
you.'

[1] Mother

Suddenly her belly tightened. Was everything ship-shape for Ba's homecoming? All details seen to? Like unwinding the reel of a film, she went over the house slowly, room by room, in her mind's eye. Nothing amiss. All in order. Each corner had been cleaned with care. But suppose . . . ? Well – her practice and the clinic really left her with no time to spare. Her mother-in-law knew it well. And those few snatched private moments, well, forget it. It's just as well Ba did not get to know.

Swiftly, suddenly, a cold shiver rose from the pit of her stomach to her throat, with a chilling reminder – the picture! The photograph of Subodh had been left undusted, with the dirty grey string of dried flowers hanging around it. She had forgotten to place a fresh wreath. And with it remained Bapuji's photograph too. Ba would of course go straight up to them, first thing on coming home.

Framed in dry dead petals, Subodh's face smiled unmoving in black and white – like the printed picture of Krishna[2] on last year's Diwali[3] card, chucked on top of a heap of discarded papers.

Shubha gripped the steering wheel hard.

The ashtray beside the telephone – had it been cleaned? Often, ever so often, in these past few days she had sat there smoking as she talked over the telephone. Suppose Ba were to ask why we needed an ashtray at all in our house? What then? Oh God! There was no time now to turn back to the house. She parked the car and went into the station.

The train arrived on time. The luggage was stacked into the car. Shubha slid behind the wheel and started

[2] Hindu god
[3] major Hindu festival

the engine and Ba got in beside her. Inching her way through milling crowds, sounding the horn intermittently, slamming the brakes on at traffic lights, she drove homeward. The driving, the traffic and the tortuous progress, she had grown used to it all now and could manage mechanically.

Ba talked. As she talked, the fatigue of the journey was shot through with the lively satisfaction that lit her face. Crisply, rapidly, Ba went about recounting the little happenings and family gossip, as she always did. Like the clickety-clack of needles knitting all the inconsequential details into the common tale of the extended Indian family. Aunt, nephew, cousin, grandmother, criss-crossing relatives gathered together to celebrate or to mourn.

The car ran on. For it had to run on. Ba's words flitted out of the window like dry leaves swept along by the afternoon breeze. Shubha was quiet. Her thoughts hovered round that ashtray near the telephone – cigarette ash wafting in the air.

Home at last. Pressing the horn twice to summon a servant, Shubha ran up the stairs, not even waiting for Ba to alight. She went straight to the telephone. No ashtray there. Damn it! She herself had put it away into the cupboard this morning.

Ba came up and headed straight for the photographs. Bapuji[4] and Subodh smiled through the film of dust. Only four months after Shubha had stepped in as a bride, father and son had died together in a road accident.

A crystal bowl decked with fresh young blossoms had dashed to the floor and shattered. Since then, like the myriad splinters of glass, were the moments of life, each

[4] Father

to be picked up, one at a time, and one by one to be put away.

Ba carefully cleaned the photographs, knelt down and touched her head to the floor. Rising she turned to Shubha, and on a faintly reproachful note asked, 'My dear, how did so much dust gather? Surely you remembered the fresh flowers and obeisance[5] every day?'

One could make excuses – of a patient being ill, of visits to be paid. But words failed Shubha. She walked out of the room slowly.

Outside, she stood leaning against the rails of the balcony. Ba, she thought, must now be busy washing and bathing. At once she was seized with an irrepressible urge. The small space between thumb and finger throbbed palpably.

She went back to the room. Ba would take a long time in her bath. She pulled the packet out with an impatient hand and lit a cigarette, taking in the first few drags hungrily. Oh God. Just to quell the restless thirst of hours . . .

One cigarette smoked, she lit another from its end. This too must be finished before Ba came out. She stood there and inhaled the smoke, deep and steady.

But how long can this go on? How long can the act be kept secret from her mother-in-law? There was the clinic, of course, where she could smoke. But Ba might just walk in there too, one day.

The sound of the bathroom door being unlatched broke her reverie. She flung the cigarette away, turned her head and peered. No, Ba was not yet back. She drew a long breath and sank down on the cane sofa.

---

[5] to bow as a mark of respect

Life. How it stretched, interminably. How inexorably the seconds tick away. No might in the world can give them a shove and push them back. Time . . .

A wave of exhaustion swept over her all at once. As if she had been plodding miles, carrying a heavy load. Now she only wanted to sit, just sit with a cigarette dangling from her listless hand.

'Don't you have to go to the clinic today?' Ba's voice reached out to her.

'I'm going,' she answered and snapped her purse shut. But she remained rooted to the sofa. The prospect of the clinic was depressing.

The faces that waited for her there would be dismal, every one of them, some bereft of all hope. To think of them was to enter that grey realm. 'I cannot eat a morsel, doctor.' 'A fever of 100° since yesterday.' 'The swellings on the feet have not gone down.' Some throats riddled with swollen glands, some tumours destined to live or to die, a ceaseless tug-of-war and unending complaints.

She heaved a sigh and just as she was about to rise and leave, Ba came in. Seeing Shubha still sitting, she drew up the cane chair opposite and sat down.

'Shubha, the wedding was really great fun, very enjoyable. Oh dear, we – now let's see, how many years since I last saw a wedding? Your wedding, of course, and after that – oh well. But Mama[6] was hurt that you did not attend. I explained to him of course. She is a doctor, I said. She has a commitment to her patients. Far be it from me to come in the way of her duty. What do you say? Isn't that so?'

An answer. One must say something now. Ba was waiting for a response. That is how it should be – some

[6] uncle on mother's side (one's mother's brother)

give and take, some conversation. Without these mundane exchanges, a home would freeze into one of those two-dimensional stills. Her voice, pitched a shade too high, broke the lengthening pause. 'How did Indu look as a bride? Was she dressed heavily for the occasion?'

'Yes indeed, dear. They had called in one of these make-up artistes, you know. A full hundred rupees she charged! But Indu looked like a doll.'

Ba pulled herself up a bit and continued, 'You know Shubha, it really makes me laugh. These modern girls are all just dolls, mere dolls. Not a jot of idealism, noble thoughts or sensibilities.'

Shubha gazed out in silence as the evening spread its shadow over the earth. She looked into the falling darkness.

'Come, now. You'll be late for work', Ba said.

She rose to her feet. Clutching the balustrade firmly in hand, she walked down the steps and out of the house. She started the car but after a moment switched off the engine. She would walk to the clinic today, she decided. It was a short distance only and she was in no mood to drive.

At the clinic, she found a large number of patients waiting for her. She took them all in at a glance. At the end of the line sat a man, neatly dressed, middle-aged. Their eyes met. An enigmatic smile played on his lips as he said, 'Have been waiting for you for ever so long.'

Shubha reacted with a start. It was not the words or voice so much, but the smile that was disquieting. A shiver of fear. As if this man could read her mind, as if he knew all, inside out.

She turned her eyes away in haste. She sat erect in her chair and answered, a trifle too loudly, a trifle too crisply. 'Sorry, I have been delayed a bit.'

One after another the patients came up to her. Some were advised to consult a specialist – for some an X-ray, for others merely an aspirin. It was all so routine. And the eyes of the man at the end of the queue somehow radiated strength to her – enhancing her capabilities, her insight, and her confidence. Yet there was that undercurrent of irritability, a weariness, an over-whelming desire just to let go .·. . !

She glanced at him. His smile hurt her, chased her about like some little whirligig, a sparkler that children light on festival nights which scatters a shower of thrill and fear round and round in its zig-zag trail.

Most of the patients had departed. It was his turn now – the last one. A cigarette. The urgent need to smoke welled up in her. Her fingers pulled out a cigarette from her purse. The man sprang up and lit it with his own lighter.

'Thank you.'

He then sat down in the chair opposite her.

'Latika has been unwell since yesterday. Doctor, would you please come?'

His voice now struck dread, like his haunting smile. His words, so mildly spoken, were a confident invitation. Beneath the words lay the phrases unspoken: 'I know . . . I know it all . . . everything.'

She stood up and said, 'Yes, let's go. We shall watch for a day or two and then maybe call in a specialist.'

He picked up Shubha's black bag, walked ahead to his car and held the door open for her. A moment's pause, then Shubha got into the front seat. He closed the door with care, walked round and got in beside her, behind the wheel.

Latika was of course not yet as well as she ought to be, but even so her condition did not quite merit a house call. Still, Shubha spent a long evening at their house. Long-ailing spinster and her bachelor brother together managed to keep the evening scintillating. She sat for a long time with the brother and sister, savouring the easy flow of conversation. The simple chatter that bounces off the walls of a house giving it the dimensions of a home. The fear of that smile had now vanished. Skeins of laughter and companionship spun a shimmering cocoon around her.

'Doctor, stay back and eat with us,' begged Latika. Shubha sprang up with a start and looked at her watch. Nine-thirty! Ba waited at home for her. She had returned . . .

'No thank you – it's late. Some other time.' She stood up.

'I had no idea of your taste in these things. I have a number of imported brands – cigarettes as well as drinks,' he said.

'Oh, no! It's only occasional . . .' Murmuring, she crossed to the telephone, called the clinic, told the compounder to close for the day. She felt agitated, scared. She had lingered too long – the laughter, the jokes – for no good reason on earth. Life. She felt alive, and yet dreaded the very touch of life, afraid to come alive.

He drove her home in his car. Lifting her black bag in his hand, he offered to carry it upstairs. But she took it from him with a 'No, thank you.'

He did not move but looked at her and said softly, 'Will you not come again, unless my sister is ill? Won't you come over just to see us? We have really enjoyed your visit. You see, we are quite alone.'

She could no longer stand there. Mumbling a formal 'Yes, of course' she quickly climbed the steps.

A cloud of sweet incense hit her at the door. She entered the living room and saw the two photographs of

Subodh and Bapuji draped with thick garlands of flowers. A bunch of incense sticks burned before them. The air hung heavy with the sweet scent. Ba sat on the floor facing the pictures, reciting the Gita.[7]

Softly, Subha crossed over to her room, put down her purse and taking the cigarette packet out, tucked it away into the cupboard. She washed her hands and face and rinsed her mouth with antiseptic. When she returned to the living room Ba had finished her recitation and was spooning the food onto the plates.

'I had to call on a patient. It got late,' she said and sat down to eat.

Ba's hand stopped still in mid-air. Shubha jumped up and prostrated herself before Subodh's photograph. Subodh was smiling at her – a distant lifeless smile framed by fresh voluptuous blossoms.

As they ate, Ba began to talk again. Shubha barely heard her. Her thoughts, her being were still in Latika's house. The faint whiff of aftershave lotion, light laughter. 'You see, we are quite alone.' His words, his eyes . . .

'We are quite alone.' She heard the words distinctly again and looked up, startled. It was Ba talking to her.

'I told your Mama, "Do not worry for us, brother, what if we are quite alone? I and my dear Shubha, we are quite apart from others".'

Shubha looked down at her plate as she ate. Ba spoke on.

'Mama was all too full of praise, dear. "Shubha is indeed a saint," he said. "Her life is like an incense stick. It burns itself to release its fragrance into the world".'

[7] Hindu holy book

Suddenly, Ba's voice ceased. Shubha looked up at her mother-in-law. A deep frown knitting her brow, Ba stared steadily into the corner opposite. She got up and walked over, and picked up something from the floor.

'Shubha, what is this?' Ba's voice cracked. Like hard dry earth. The barren sunbaked earth cracks, willy-nilly, along deep jagged fissures.

With thin trembling fingers Ba held up the burnt-out stub of a cigarette.

Translated by Sima Sharma

Murli Das Melwani

The Bhorwani Marriage

'Do you have a good house in hand, *Maharaj*?'[1] asked the plump woman who intercepted me as I was leaving on my daily rounds.

I invited her into my house.

'For your son or daughter?'

The question was irrelevant; obviously it was for the scarecrow of a girl that accompanied her. But I asked it in order to gain time to assess what this party was worth. The woman was dressed in a plain cream-coloured nylon georgette saree. She was not wearing any jewellery either. But that indicated nothing. Mothers these days were shrewd. They didn't want to immediately reveal how well off they were lest the match-maker or the boy's party or both should make fantastic demands. These women bargained hard.

The girl was wearing a bizarre hair-do and I imagine that she kept her head tilted lest it should get upset. She was wearing an embroidered saree – at 7 o'clock in the morning. She must have left bed around 4 am or so to dress like that. Hell, these marriageable girls think that if they impress me they've impressed the 'bride-groom'. They should know that I'm going to inflict my sales-talk on the other party whether personally I'm impressed or

[1] in this story, a man who is paid by parents to find a suitable marriage partner for their son or daughter. Marriage is largely influenced by parents for it is families that marry each other. He needs to consider issues of caste, character, education, dowry and astrological charts.

not. I'm more interested in how much I'm getting out of the whole business.

'The girl now,' said the woman, indicating the show-piece. 'A son later.'

She was one of the smarter ones; trying to tempt me with the possibility of a bigger commission if I performed my first commission satisfactorily.

'Of course, I know a few parties,' I said non-committingly.

'We've come from . . .' She mentioned the name of some far-off place.

I wasn't impressed. 'Oh, yes. They keep flying in from Jamaica and Biafra, from Indonesia and Africa. Flying in from Japan and Hong Kong has become an everday affair. And they all ask for Atu Maharaj.'

Yes, I'm proud of my notoriety – the other maharajs in the trade would have said 'fame'. Modesty, in fact, is one of my shortcomings. I'm not as smart as they are with the result that though I do more than the others I earn much less than them.

'Please arrange something quickly. The noise of your Bombay traffic is bursting our ear-drums.'

Just then my wife entered from our second, and only other room, and for the next few minutes the two women discussed the all-important subject of Bombay traffic. I still hadn't been able to assess the standard of the party. So I asked, as inoffensively as possible:

'How much are you prepared to give?'

'Depending on the house you get us.'

This answer was classic in its diplomacy. The woman was smarter than I imagined. I therefore made an indirect approach.

'There's a good party, but they live far and I'll have to go by taxi . . . .'

'We will pay all your taxi bills.'

Her answer meant that she would reward me sufficiently. I was satisfied, perhaps even a little embarrassed
for having resorted to indirect means to elicit information. But the difference between me and the other
maharajas was that whereas they would straightaway
have demanded, grabbed at and pocketed a five *rupee*
note for taxi fare I left it for later.

'Now who is this party?' The woman wasn't going to
let me off easily. 'Tell me so that I can write to my
daughter's father. He hasn't come with us.' Fathers
looked after their business; daughters were none of their
business.

'There are two or three,' I said to ward her off.

I promised to call on her and took down the necessary
particulars. They were Bhorwanis from Uruguay. They
owned two factories manufacturing baby garments and
had 1,255 men in their employ. By marriage they were
connected to the Rotwanis of Rourkela, the Relsinghanis
of Ankara, the Kalachandanis of Kohima, and a
number of other well known families scattered all over
the globe. Uruguay was a new country to me and I
decided to ask my twelve-year-old son – as I so often
did – to find out from his geography teacher where this
monstrosity was located. Really, the places Indians
have gone to!

Having got rid of the party, I set out on my daily
round, late by over an hour. I had to return to the
Balanis' (of Quebec) son's horoscope because the
young man was leaving shortly – after having seen and
rejected 22 girls. He promised to come next year. The
Balani business had been a dead loss for me. All that I
had been able to get out of them were a few pure
French chiffon sarees for my wife. Then I had to call on
the Casanis to fix a date for their daughter's first
'viewing' by the Budhwani boy. By the time it was 2

o'clock I would be at the Gawklanis', just in time for the midday meal with them; the grandmother cooks the best 'kari' I've tasted anywhere. My afternoon nap would be with the Keswani family at Colaba. Then I would have to find out what the Karnanis of the Fiji islands had thought about my proposal for the Basarmani girl from Gibraltar. The evening would find me attending the Varowani marriage at the Jai Hind College Hall. Not because I was officiating – Rishu Maharaj would be performing the ceremony. I was going chiefly to point out the Motwani girl (BA from London) to the Sippymalani boy (drawing 5,000 francs in France). I would be home earliest by 10 pm. A largely thankless job.

Thoughts of the Bhorwani girl from . . . the new country . . . occupied me the whole of the next day. She was thin and dark. Boys nowadays demand a white skin even if the features of the girl are not striking. No doubt her thinness could be to her advantage. Boys insisted on this feature even though they allowed themselves to puff out in all directions and let their excess baggage show through their clothes. But this girl was exceptionally thin.

I could of course show her to the Charwani boy from Shillong in far away Assam where meat formed the staple diet, snakes were served as delicacies on festive days and head-hunting was the favourite pastime of the people. Parents must be mad to offer their daughters to such parties. Yet this clown had seen and rejected 67 girls. In fact, he had rented a suite at the Royal Hotel on an yearly basis.

Then I could suggest the Furtani boy. But his requirements were such that no maharaj could hope to satisfy. God himself would have to create a special girl for him. The Parnani family from America was not a bad proposition. The boy was an engineer and he was not particular about the type of girl he married. His parents were the ones who were creating all those headaches for me. Ah! and my wife had told me that a certain Ringhawani party had only yesterday arrived from Oslo (must remember to ask my son where that was!). I weighed what my gains from either match would be, before I re-approached them.

I was sure I could get round the Engineer Parnani, but his mother? She was asking for what we call 'everything' – two diamond rings, two diamond ear-rings, two diamond bangles and a diamond necklace plus the usual sets of clothes and gifts to the near and dear ones. I was confident that if the Bhorwani woman was satisfied about the Parnani family she would be willing to satisfy their demands. I called on her a few days later.

'Even a glimpse of yours is so rare and expensive these days,' said Mrs Bhorwani in the polite way of greeting.

I told her how busy I was and to what expense I had gone to locate a party suitable for her princess of a daughter. I gave her a list of the expenses I had incurred, not forgetting to add that taxis these days seldom used meters and the drivers charged fancy fares. She gave me more than the amount I mentioned, and I told her about the Parnani boy.

'He looks like a king. And he behaves like a king.'

The daughter who was hovering around pretended not to have heard me.

'But his mother. She wants' – a calculated pause – 'everything'.

For the next half hour I used all the diplomacy and powers of persuasion at my command to overcome her arguments. Finally she said:

'If the boy is as good as you say, we will give well.' Smart as she was she wouldn't commit herself to 'everything'.

I satisfied the Parnani woman with the references of the Bhorwani family, their background, lineage and connections by marriage. I added:

'The girl is a princess in her slimness. Even the lotus with its stalk would blush before her. Boys nowadays demand slimness like hers.'

The Parnani woman agreed to allow her son to see the Bhorwani girl. I went about making the necessary preparations. This was the season of marriages, and we maharajs use these occasions to display and parade all our prospects, male and female. A marriage I had succeeded in arranging was in the offing (remember the mad Melwanis in the mango business at Malda?), and I proposed to use it for this occasion.

Amid all the glitter and noise and flashily dressed guests, my wife pointed out the girl to the Parnani boy. He peered through the thick glasses, pointed to the wrong girl and said, 'Will do.' When my wife corrected him he peered again and again said, 'Will do.'

The very next day I went to collect the horoscopes and my pending taxi fare from both the parties (the same amount from both). Usually it was the boy's 'no' that would squash a promising development, but in this case the horoscopes threatened to create difficulties. They did not match. I reported this matter to Mrs Bhorwani first. She was distressed. But I reassured her that if we performed a small *puja*[2] – a little expensive perhaps – any unhealthy effects arising from improperly conjoined stars would be mitigated. Indeed, the more the offerings (preferably financial), the greater was the

[2] Hindu worship in which offerings are made

likelihood of the stars falling into positions beneficial to both the parties. The woman didn't mind the expense involved – indeed, urged me to perform the most expensive puja I could think of! But the Parnani father was adamant. 'No marriage if horoscopes don't match,' he said repeatedly in English. So the Bhorwani-Parnani negotiations ended there.

The Charwani boy from Shillong and the Furtani prince would say 'no'. So I turned my thoughts to the Ringhawani party. The boy didn't speak much, hence appeared to be a sensible sort of fellow. Both the parties agreed on what was to be given and accepted. The preliminary viewing at a marriage was gone through without a hitch. The horoscopes also matched. The Bhorwani father was called over; he was constrained to leave his business because he was assured that something definite was brewing.

My house was chosen as the venue for the 'viewing' by the boy's mother and sundry other female relatives. Mrs Bhorwani thoughtfully saw to it that I bought enough sweets and soft drinks to entertain everybody.

'The girl is rather thin,' remarked one of the women in the Ringhawani group, popping a huge Asoo sweet in her mouth. She spoke in what may have appeared to be a whisper, but was loud enough for all to hear.

'Perhaps she doesn't get enough to eat,' added another, addressing the first in a whisper meant for everybody's ear.

The girl pretented not to hear, buried as she was in a well-thumbed magazine. I kept a number of magazines handy for such occasions.

'Poor thing, even her collar bones are showing.'

My wife is always tense when such remarks are freely exchanged, but I see it as our inverted way of expressing approval.

My reading was correct. The women, impressed by all the jewellery that was being offered, said that they would ask the boy to 'speak' to the girl. The final round in the negotiations had been reached. The women shrewdly threw the ball in the boy's court. Since, they argued, it was he who would have to spend a lifetime with the girl. But their motive was to absolve themselves of all responsibility: if afterwards the boy complained that he had been saddled with the wrong partner, they could turn round and tell him that they had merely given their opinion, at most advised him, but the decision had been his; he could have refused when he still had the chance.

The inevitable Apollo seaface was chosen as the meeting place. The Bhorwani family, as is usual on such occasions, was there before the boy's party arrived. The boy was wearing a mustard coloured trouser and a magenta shirt. In our days such colours were seen only at the circus. Some sort of manipulation, very casual, saw to it that everybody spoke with everybody else, leaving the boy and girl free to speak to each other. We walked up and down the seaface a number of times. A few strollers stopped and stared at us. On such occasions the boy and girl are too over-awed, the others too preoccupied, and I too anxious about a hopeful outcome to be conscious of the humour of the parade.

I overheard the Bhorwani girl say something about Bombay traffic. I am thankful to this feature of city's life for providing these two young people an opportunity to discover that they held similar views on life.

The next – and logical – step was for both the parties to entertain each other to tea at the Taj Mahal Hotel looming over the waterfront. The bearer placed the menu in the centre of the table and for a few minutes no one noticed it. The bearer then reminded no one in

particular: 'Menu, *sahib*.'[3] At which I placed it before
the boy. All courtesy, he slid it towards the girl. The
girl shyly pushed it to her mother. The mother out of
deference placed it before the boy's mother. The menu
must have made two rounds of the table before someone
ordered chutney sandwiches and coffee. I imagine the
bearer had fallen asleep. Chutney not being readily
available, the sandwiches arrived after a long time. The
pauses were filled by reminiscences relating to sundry
features of Bombay's everyday life, its traffic not
excluded.

Since everyone's views were similar everyone believed
that the other would make a good relative. When my
wife asked the boy whether he found the girl suitable he
nodded his assent.

Preparations began to be made for the marriage. The
woman who had found the girl too thin now found
virtue in these very proportions: what fairy she was
compared to the shapeless creatures one came across
these days! Collar bones visible over blouses were the
latest in fashion – according to a difficult-to-recall-at-
the-moment fashion authority in France. An older
relative praised the girl for fasting with such faith and
fervour for a good husband as to reduce herself to a
skeleton. All the new relations were happy with each
other. They insisted during the marriage on being
photographed again and again sharing a bottle of Coca-
Cola out of two straws. Even in the movie that was shot
then, they wanted to demonstrate their happiness in
this manner. I was happy also, for bringing two young
people together for life, and also because I earned three
thousand rupees from each party. I didn't bargain but
took what was gladly given to me. Considering that a

[3] Sir

mere *lakh*[4] and a half was blown over the pomp and show I was satisfied with what I was given. One must be grateful for the crumbs that life throws one's way.

---

[4] 100,000 (rupees)

Suniti Namjoshi

The Bride

Once upon a time there was a proud young prince, and he had reason to be proud. He was heir to the kingdom, he was handsome and healthy, he had been extremely well educated, and all the social graces that could reasonably be taught had been carefully inculcated. What was more, his father was a king, and his father's father, and his father before that, so that his right to rule was undisputed. Now, when it was time for this young man to marry, he said to his father. 'Father, you have always said that only the best was fit for me. I have the best falcons, and the best hounds and the best stallions in all the world. But where will you find a bride who is worthy of me?' The king didn't think that this would be much of a problem. He had contests instituted throughout the kingdom. There were contests for beauty, and contests for strength, and contests for knowledge and intelligence and wit, and there were skill-testing contests for all sorts of things such as archery and music. When the tests were done, the winners of the contests were presented to the prince. He looked them over. Their credentials were good. Indeed, he began to be afraid that some of their credentials were better than his. 'These women have excelled,' he said to his father, 'but they seem to be lacking in the womanly qualities.' 'Well, of course,' said his father. 'I have weeded these out. You can now choose from those who did not compete.'

Padma Perera

Too Late for Anger

My sister always said the crockery in the Kirit household smelled of eggs. The Kirit sisters smelled, too, but of perfume – heavy and overpowering perfume, perhaps logically, since they were heavy and overpowering themselves. The brothers reeked of tobacco, occasionally of liquor. And the last time I visited them there was another smell, the most disturbing of all – a dank odour of decay that carried with it the echoing footsteps of the only two Kirits now left in the old house.

We had known the Kirits, as I will call them, as far back as I can remember. They were family friends – the eldest brother, Raj, a colleague of my father's; and the youngest sister, Lena, already a teacher while I was still in middle school. The father had been a doctor. Old Man Kirit, he was called, a familiar and well-loved figure in the south. His rise had been phenomenal. He came from a family of fisherfolk on the west coast – a penniless youth arriving in the city, working his way through night school and then the medical college, winning scholarships, gathering friends along with degrees, marrying a clever, ambitious, 'useful' wife, whom he loved, and buying a big house in what had been the most exclusive section of Madras.

When I saw it one day last year, buses rumbled past, jostled by rickshaws and clattering horse-drawn *jutkas*;[1]

---

[1] horse-drawn carriages

there were big shops and little wayside stalls selling *betel* leaves[2] and spices, and always the hurrying thrum of humanity on the pavements. But the house was set well back from the road and the noises were muffled, caught between the close-leaved branches of the tamarind trees that lined the drive and somehow sheltered the big house and what it held. That day, I found the garden lying shrivelled and bare. The drive was ill-kept, a few flowerpots wilted on the front steps, and the halls and rooms seemed to be furnished with spaces – unyielding, tangible spaces that told you they had once been filled.

The floor, too; beneath the dust, the marble mosaic gleamed dully, of better times, when the mother had insisted on its being swept and washed twice a day. Her portrait (painted when she was still a middle-aged woman) hung on the wall of the living room – a sombre thing of greys and greens merging into vague surrounding blackness. Yet the dark did not overshadow her, dominate her; instead, it was as if she created the dark. I shivered a little, looking at it, and wondered how well the artist had known her. How could he have sensed the darkening when the house was full of sunlight? When the daughters were young and beautiful and the sons reputedly brilliant and sought-after? Raj and Jairaj, slapping their tennis rackets across their knees, running down the stairs laughing. And the girls with their floating pastel saris, their absurdly rhyming names: Meena and Nina and Lena. The only odd one out had been Sheela. She was slight and dark and quiet, painfully conscious of the cast in her left eye, a shadow behind her mother, helping to run the house, supervise in the kitchen, see to the meals. We never saw her with the others at picnics and parties and concerts – not even

[2] large leaves used to wrap around spices, eaten after a meal

in the library or on the beach. She always stayed behind, a silent, soft-footed wraith moving through the empty rooms when the others had gone out. My sister and I called her Cinderella and thought it a pity that Madras was too warm for fires. She would have made a perfect picture sweeping the hearth. And besides, it would be fun playing fairy godmother to her, devising ways to transform her into a vision of grace.

We pitied her with the extravagant loyalty of youth, but never thought to pity the others. Weren't they forever going out, enjoying themselves, walking the earth like large and beautiful goddesses in their exquisite clothes? We never realised that they were always formidably flanked by their parents – the mother grim and compelling (her daughters must always have the best) and the father booming pleasantries left and right, thumping people on the back, being thumped in return. We didn't know until years later their almost neurotic fear of being talked about. They were the Kirit girls and they had to remain pure and lovely, untouched alike by rumour or the bazaar smells that were already beginning to creep into the gracious neighbourhood.

Meena was the eldest of the girls, the most slender and serene. Her friends called her the Waiting Madonna, because her dreamy dark eyes always seemed to be fixed on Wednesday week – or any other day in the middle distance, towards which she poised her whole being and even pitched the tone of her voice, low but carrying. But whatever it was she was waiting for was large enough to include her immediate surroundings in its direction; if you happened to be in her line of vision, she noticed you, was exquisitely courteous and attentive, and acquired the reputation of being a wonderful hostess. Yet there remained the remoteness, the waiting, and it made her a strangely restful person to be with. When she and Lena graduated from the university with honours and prepared to leave for England, we thought she had come to what she was waiting for: travel, education, widening perspectives – all that a trip abroad held. They were away three years, Lena reading English at Oxford. Meena at the London School of Economics. What those three years did for them I do not know; presumably, what study abroad does for most Indian youth. If they developed the intellectual schizophrenia that afflicts Westernised Easterners, or found it difficult to fit into their appointed niches as daughters of the family when they returned, they did not show it. And Meena still waited.

Meanwhile, the other sister, Nina, had enrolled in the local medical college, riding on the wave of her father's success but proving herself adequately bright and more than adequately attractive. 'Carries on the tradition, eh?' Old Man Kirit boomed, hugely pleased. He took her with him everywhere he went, while Sheela stayed at home, depending more and more on her mother, shrinking away from all other human contact.

'It isn't *good* for her,' Raj said to us, roused out of his usual cheerful imperturbability. 'I worry about her. I worry terribly.' Raj was closest to us, meeting us most often and discussing his problems with my parents. He didn't look worried. Raj had inherited his father's bonhomie, claiming to be waiting for my sister and me to grow up so he could marry one or the other of us. 'Give me Mangalore girls every time, hey?' he would say, pinching my cheek. 'Famous for two things, Mangalore: the splendour of its landscape and the beauty of its women.' We wished we weren't from Mangalore, but smiled politely and agreed in private that he was being rather ridiculous, constantly talking about the pretty girls he would like to marry.

As it turned out, Raj never married. A few months after the girls returned to India, Old Man Kirit and his wife were killed in a motor accident. When my mother came home from the funeral, I heard her say, 'This will break poor Sheela unless the rest of them rally around her. Already she looks like death.' And my father replied, abruptly for him, 'They've always been close – I hope they get more independent now.' But the Kirits only grew closer still.

Raj postponed marriage. First, the girls had to be married, 'settled'. The responsibility devolved upon him as the eldest, and besides, Jairaj, after the prescribed period of mourning, was too busy being a playboy. He joined a foreign business firm, spent his Saturday afternoons at the racecourse, threw himself with éclat into the cocktail-party crowd, and took to drinking a good deal. 'Women, too,' the gossips muttered darkly. Whether that was prompted by malice or fact, Jairaj was undoubtedly attractive to women. A shooting accident that injured his leg had left him with a limp; he rode and swam well, and could be articulate in a brittle fashion that passed for wit. 'Stands there blowing cigarette smoke in your face and raising his left eyebrow, and the girls fall for it every time,' Raj reported gloomily. 'Romantic as hell.'

Soon after this, Jairaj offered the tentative suggestion that he take a flat in town, but the idea evaporated of its own accord. Perhaps the dead mother's disapproval glaring down at him from the wall or his own guilt at deserting the family proved too strong. And he was comfortable enough in the big house; Raj was an easygoing head of the family, making no demands on the others, only upon himself.

The girls were working now. Meena and Leena became decorative additions to the staff of a women's college, and Nina an intern in the city's new hospital. But it was tacitly agreed that this state of affairs was temporary. Career women were still something out of the ordinary, and the Kirit girls were avid for the conventional, the 'safe' life – a placid marriage and then an inevitable family strongly bulwarked by the oh-so-solid social structure. They came home straight from work, to avoid the least breath of scandal, for girls who acquired the wrong kind of reputation rarely acquired the right kind of husband.

And then there was Sheela. Lovingly and slowly, her brothers and sisters tried to chip off the layers of numbness that enveloped her. Listlessly, she allowed them to do what they liked. They took her to concerts and parties and the theatre, but she endured each as if it were an infliction rather than an entertainment. They brought her plenty to read, but she sat at the window, gazing out, with the book lying open and unread on her lap. They took her shopping and bought her fashionable ensembles, but the new clothes looked vaguely apologetic on Sheela, as if they were begging her pardon for being there.

'I don't know *what* to do with the girl,' Raj finally complained to my mother, in desperation. 'Nothing seems to work. *She* won't work, either. Or study.'

My mother thought for a moment and then said, with apparent irrelevance, 'How about the Temple Festival at Shivanur? We're going – would you like to join us?'

So we all went together.

Shivanur is a seacoast village about thirty miles south of Madras. Every twelve years, pilgrims from all over the country gather there to attend its famous Temple Festival. The temple itself stands on the seashore, where the sea and the sculptured stone have been looking at each other for the last fifteen hundred years. Legend has it that the Ganga,[3] flowing through a secret underground source, joins the sea here once in twelve years. Then prayers are said at dawn and the pilgrims bathe in the sea; the ritual worship of *puja* is performed in the temple and the poor are fed.

All day the village is alive with the temple fair. We saw potters with their earthenware, farmers with their grain, bangle sellers, little boys selling baskets, whole families of weavers squatting behind the vivid silks flung enticingly across their stalls to attract the pilgrims. There were trinkets for women and brightly painted wooden toys for children, and the objects used for worship – beautiful old lamps and bells, rosaries made of dried *rudrakshi*[4] berries, the sacred texts bound in cloth, fruits and flowers, sandalwood, camphor, and incense.

The Kirit women, grown up as they were, seemed almost as excited as my sister and I. They bought us some glass bangles, and when the bangle seller slipped the tinkling blues and greens on our wrists, Meena tried them on too, quoting Sarojini Naidu's poem about 'rainbow-tinted circles of delight'. Nina lost herself in the silk shops, to emerge half an hour later with shimmering folds of tangerine and gold, but Lena could not buy anything, because she had given away all her money to the beggars who throng every Hindu place of pilgrimage. And apparently my mother had known what she was talking about, for here at last Sheela came to life – slowly at first, until she worshipped at the temple and mingled with the crowds at the fair, caught in a throbbing, insistent new rhythm so utterly unlike

[3] the Ganges, the river believed to be holy by Hindus
[4] tropical fruit

the measured pace of existence in the big house that she surrendered in spite of herself.

'I'd like to come here when all the people have left,' Meena announced suddenly. We were drinking tender-coconut milk on the beach beside the temple courtyard. 'I'd like to live here always. Just sketch and bathe and be; lie on the sands or here in the shade of the temple, listening to the wind in the palms, soaking in *centuries* of peace. And live on tender-coconuts all day.' Jairaj murmured something cynical about indigestion, but she wasn't listening. She turned to her older brother and her eyes were suddenly brilliant. 'Raj, I've decided,' she said. 'It's yes.'

That was how we knew that Raj's efforts at hunting for a brother-in-law had proved successful. 'The boy,' as everyone referred to him, was pronounced entirely satisfactory. He was from the same linguistic community, had completed his education abroad and so did not mind a 'foreign-returned' bride with more academic degrees than was seemly for a woman; also, he was a pilot in the Air Force, suitably dashing and suitably well connected. Meena had met him twice. 'You know,' she admitted later, 'It does become rather an impasse in this society of ours. You can't get engaged to a person until you know him well enough, and you can't know him well enough until you get engaged to him. Anyway, I've decided ·as best I could under the circum-stances . . .' and her eyes were brilliant again.

Watching Meena in those days was almost frightening. Her radiance had a perilous edge. She was so beautiful that you couldn't look at her for long; you turned away from the naked joy in her eyes. Now Meena had no more need to wait.

Her fiancé stayed in Madras for a week and then went north for special military training. Raj kept congratulating himself on his success and consulting my mother about preparations to be made for the wedding. Meena's horoscope was sent to the astrologer, and word came back that the wedding would have to be postponed for six months, since both 'the boy' and 'the girl' were passing through what he called 'an uncertain period'. Meena herself, seeming not the slightest bit uncertain, went shopping for her trousseau with her sisters.

But it was only Sheela she took with her on the trip to the silk weavers' town, where saris were cheaper than in the city. It rained that weekend, and both girls were drenched and came home with colds which worsened to a serious chill, spelling pleurisy. Meena, being the stronger of the two, was recovering slowly, but Sheela grew thin and feverish and bright-eyed, and before the end of the month Raj brought bad news. Her lungs were badly affected; the doctors said she had to be removed to a sanatorium.

What came next happened with bewildering rapidity. Sheela was moved to the sanatorium, and a week later Meena's engagement was broken by her fiancé's family. With tuberculosis in the family, they said, You Never Know.

Raj came to us with haggard eyes. 'I haven't told her yet,' he said. 'I couldn't. Not when she's ill. And she keeps waiting for the mail and wondering why there are no letters . . . .'

'But *why*?' my sister cried indignantly. She had always loved Meena best. 'Why should they do a thing like that? Illness isn't a crime –'

'Here it apparently is,' Raj replied bitterly. 'Marriage is a breeding institution, and they want to make sure the production machine is in working order.' We had never seen him so angry.

'And what about *him*?' we persisted, almost equally angry. 'Why doesn't *he* do something about it? He loved – well, *liked* her, didn't he?'

Raj stopped us with a gesture. 'Because he hasn't the guts. Because our country today breeds namby-pamby Milquetoasts, with neither the discipline of the old nor the vigour of the new – they haven't the faith to live with duty and haven't the courage to live without it. They're a living celebration of the apron string.'

'And Meena?'

'I don't know – this sort of thing pretty well shuts up all other avenues. She's caught in the same chasm between the old and the new. Our girls are given the education and ideals to believe in freedom, but never the circumstances and encouragement to carry it out, to live what they believe. It's a sham all around . . .' He paused in his tirade and then touched my cheek gently. 'You, too, little ones. Perhaps the next generation will escape – but you'll get it. And my other sisters, God knows what will happen to them.'

Soon he did know. Lena, watching the tragic, empty-eyed shell of a human being that Meena had become, announced that she would have none of these arranged marriages if this was the way they ended. And, trying to shake off the old dread of being talked about, she joined a group of teachers who were taking a trip to Kashmir during the summer vacation. Our family had moved north that summer, so we saw her on her way back. She was with another professor, a thin, eager, dark man with restless hands, a voluble tongue, and the high intellectual forehead of the South-Indian *Brahman*.[5] They came to tea and he talked all the time, handling

[5] the highest caste in the Hindu caste system

abstract concepts as palpably as he handled the cup in his hand. Lena looked and smiled and listened, and then, just before they left, she drew my mother aside with a swift, shy gesture unexpectedly touching in someone with her usual assurance. They hoped to be married when they returned to Madras, she said, after Gopal's parents had given their permission and blessing.

There was no blessing. We heard about the scene later. The father had raged and stamped and threatened to throw his son out of the house. The mother had cowered and wept in a corner. 'Marry a girl from the fisher-people!' he had roared, his sacred thread[6] quivering in indignation, the caste mark on his forehead drawn together in a thunderous frown. 'How *dare* you pollute the air in this house with a blasphemous suggestion like that –' It was all rather like the classic situation in one of our third-rate films, we thought. Of course, the young intellectual would walk out of the house and marry the girl he loved.

We waited – the mother had begged for time. And the father used it. Barely a week later, Gopal was told that he was to be married to a remote cousin thrice removed, a well-born young woman with no highfalutin foreign ideas and no more education than was good for her. It was all arranged; the date had been set, down to the auspicious moment when he would clasp wedding *tali*[7] around the girl's neck, and the invitations had already been sent out. It was too late to change anything. If Gopal did, it would spell disaster not only to the girl but to the entire clan. They would never live

---

[6] a cotton thread first placed over his head as a boy & resting from his shoulder to opposite hip

[7] ornamental neckware

down the disgrace, and the sin would be upon his head. So, given the choice of ruining two lives, Gopal chose to ruin Lena's.

'Perhaps,' Raj wrote us savagely, 'the young intellectual feels that her degree will keep her warm at night.'

With this, the Kirits drew even closer together. To Sheela, whose condition had been deteriorating, Lena's misfortune was the last straw. She grew steadily weaker, and died of a haemorrhage towards the end of the year. The house was quiet now; there was no sound of laughter, no sound of the boys running lightly down the stairs. Raj gave up all idea of marriage. As long as he was alive, he said quietly and without dramatics, he would have to look after his sisters, they might be financially independent and academically qualified, but they were women and they needed protection. Jairaj, too, continuing on his usual carefree course, remained a bachelor. Lena and Meena taught, and came home straight from work again, not because they feared scandal now but because the college held nothing to interest them particularly. Lena served on committees, more from a resigned sense of duty than anything else. And Meena had stopped entertaining long ago. They grew fat and rather apathetic, with pasty complexions and an addiction to heavy perfume and florid printed chiffons. Nina went to Hyderabad to work in a hospital, married a wastrel much younger than herself, and spent the rest of her youth and health and sanity supporting him.

We did not see the Kirits for many years. Our own lives were catching up with us; we had not time to visit the south. My sister settled in Bombay, and when I won a scholarship to study abroad, she thought it apropos to remind me about them.

'It doesn't pay being a deviant here,' she said wryly. 'Example, the Kirits.'

'Especially when you don't *want* to be one,' I agreed. 'Example, the Kirits.'

And we spoke of the mother and the girls' tutored horror of being 'different,' and of how different they had eventually become from most of their contemporaries.

When my father went south for a conference, he called on them, and came away with an impression of such intense, even suffocating closeness that, he said, the very house had seemed airless. Jairaj was in bed; his injured leg had started to give him serious trouble and made him a querulous invalid. The sisters took turns nursing him. Lena had been offered a fellowship in a European university, but she declined it – Jairaj had to be looked after, and besides, Meena would miss her, Meena liked feminine company in the house. A few months earlier, an elderly widower had timidly approached the empty-eyed but still beautiful Meena with a proposal of marriage, only to be met with an indifferent refusal. Something had broken in her, she said; she couldn't rouse herself to care for a stranger again. Besides, Jairaj needed nursing and Lena would be lonely without her. Raj watched over them all, getting thin and wizened, his laughter and loquacity dwindling with the years.

'They're trying to *preserve* each other,' my sister summed up, in a muffled voice, to acknowledge partial truth. 'They *have* to, they've no choice. And yet you can't do that. Human beings aren't jam.'

It was last year that I made my own visit to Madras, with my mother. When I saw Lena and Raj, I remembered what my sister had said. The Kirits had sacrificed their individual selves for the family until there was no family left. No one else left. Meena and Jairaj had died, and Nina, once a capable doctor, now shut herself up in a room at the back of the house; her years with the wastrel had proved too much for her. Raj called it a nervous breakdown, and Lena could not bear to think of her sister in a sanatorium. 'They've offered me that fellowship again,' Lena mentioned in passing, 'and of course I've refused once more. I'm needed at home.'

They stood at the front door, waving goodbye when we left. Walking down the drive, I tried to tie up all that had happened with the inexplicable quietness in Lena's eyes. 'Look out!' my mother cried suddenly, jolting me out of my thoughts. I had almost stumbled against one of the betel sellers, who was squatting by the hedge, preparing to pitch a tent there for the night. He had done it for years now, he said. The people in the big house raised no objection. And he smiled a little and looked at the house, its paint peeling and its railings drunkenly askew, old and dilapidated behind the tamarind trees.

Attia Hosain

The First Party

After the dimness of the verandah, the bewildering brightness of the room made her stumble against the unseen doorstep. Her nervousness edged towards panic, and the darkness seemed a forsaken friend, but her husband was already steadying her into the room.

'My wife,' he said in English, and the alien sounds softened the awareness of this new relationship.

The smiling, tall woman came towards them with outstretched hands and she put her own limply into the other's firm grasp.

'How d'you do?' said the woman.

'How d'you do?' said the fat man beside her.

'I am very well, thank you,' she said in the low voice of an uncertain child repeating a lesson. Her shy glance avoided their eyes.

They turned to her husband, and in the warm current of their friendly ease she stood coldly self-conscious.

'I hope we are not too early,' her husband said.

'Of course not; the others are late. Do sit down.'

She sat on the edge of the big chair, her shoulders drooping, nervously pulling her sari over her head as the weight of its heavy gold embroidery pulled it back.

'What will you drink?' the fat man asked her.

'Nothing, thank you.'

'Cigarette?'

'No, thank you.'

Her husband and the tall woman were talking about her, she felt sure. Pin-points of discomfort pricked her and she smiled to hide them.

The woman held a wineglass in one hand and a cigarette in the other. She wondered how it felt to hold a cigarette with such self-confidence; to flick the ash with such assurance. The woman had long nails, pointed and scarlet. She looked at her own – unpainted, cut carefully short – wondering how anyone could eat, work, wash with those claws dipped in blood. She drew her sari over her hands, covering her rings and bracelets, noticing the other's bare wrists, like a widow's.

'Shy little thing, isn't she, but charming,' said the woman as if soothing a frightened child.

'She'll get over it soon. Give me time,' her husband laughed. She heard him and blushed, wishing to be left unobserved and grateful for the diversion when other guests came in.

She did not know whether she was meant to stand up when they were being introduced, and shifted uneasily in the chair, half rising; but her husband came and stood by her, and by the pressure of his hand on her shoulder she knew she must remain sitting.

She was glad when polite formality ended and they forgot her for their drinks, their cigarettes, their talk and laughter. She shrank into her chair, lonely in her strangeness yet dreading approach. She felt curious eyes on her and her discomfort multiplied them. When anyone came and sat by her she smiled in cold defence, uncertainty seeking refuge in silence, and her brief answers crippled conversation. She found the bilingual patchwork distracting, and its pattern, familiar to others, with allusions and references unrelated to her own experiences, was distressingly obscure. Overheard light chatter appealing to her woman's mind brought no relief of understanding. Their different stresses made even talk of dress and appearance sound unfamiliar. She could not understand the importance of relating clothes to time and place and not just occasion; nor their preoccupation with limbs and bodies, which should be covered, and not face and features alone. They made problems about things she took for granted.

Her bright rich clothes and heavy jewellery oppressed her when she saw the simplicity of their clothes. She wished she had not dressed so, even if it was the custom, because no one seemed to care for customs, or even know them, and looked at her as if she were an object on display. Her discomfort changed to uneasy defiance, and she stared at the strange creatures around her. But her swift eyes slipped away in timid shyness if they met another's.

Her husband came at intervals that grew longer with a few gay words, or a friend to whom he proudly presented 'My wife.' She noticed the never-empty glass in his hand, and the smell of his breath, and from shock and distress she turned to disgust and anger. It was wicked, it was sinful to drink, and she could not forgive him.

She could not make herself smile any more but no one noticed and their unconcern soured her anger. She did not want to be disturbed and was tired of the persistent 'Will you have a drink?', 'What will you drink?', 'Sure you won't drink?' It seemed they objected to her not drinking, and she was confused by this reversal of values. She asked for a glass of orange juice and used it as protection, putting it to her lips when anyone came near.

They were eating now, helping themselves from the table by the wall. She did not want to leave her chair, and wondered if it was wrong and they would notice she was not eating. In her confusion she saw a girl coming towards her, carrying a small tray. She sat up stiffly and took the proffered plate with a smile.

'Do help yourself,' the girl said and bent forward. Her light sari slipped from her shoulder and the tight red silk blouse outlined each high breast. She pulled her own sari closer round her, blushing. The girl, unaware, said, 'Try this sandwich, and the olives are good.'

She had never seen an olive before but did not want to admit it, and when she put it in her mouth she wanted to spit it out. When no one was looking, she slipped it under her chair, then felt sure someone had seen her and would find it.

The room closed in on her with its noise and smoke. There was now the added harsh clamour of music from the radiogram. She watched, fascinated, the movement of the machine as it changed records; but she hated the shrieking and moaning and discordant noises it hurled at her. A girl walked up to it and started singing, swaying her hips. The bare flesh of her body showed through the thin net of her drapery below the high line of her short tight bodice.

She felt angry again. The disgusting, shameless hussies, bold and free with men, their clothes adorning nakedness not hiding it, with their painted false mouths, that short hair that looked like the mad woman's whose hair was cropped to stop her pulling it out.

She fed her resentment with every possible fault her mind could seize on, and she tried to deny her lonely unhappiness with contempt and moral passion. These women who were her own kind, yet not so, were wicked, contemptible, grotesque mimics of the foreign ones among them for whom she felt no hatred because from them she expected nothing better.

She wanted to break those records, the noise from which they called music.

A few couples began to dance when they had rolled aside the carpet. She felt a sick horror at the way the men held the women, at the closeness of their bodies, their vulgar suggestive movements. That surely was the extreme limit of what was possible in the presence of others. Her mother had nearly died in childbirth and not moaned lest the men outside hear her voice, and she, her child, had to see this exhibition of . . . her outraged modesty put a leash on her thoughts.

This was an assault on the basic precept by which her convictions were shaped, her life was controlled. Not against touch alone, but sound and sight, had barriers been raised against man's desire.

A man came and asked her to dance and she shrank back in horror, shaking her head. Her husband saw her and called out as he danced, 'Come on, don't be shy; you'll soon learn.'

She felt a flame of anger as she looked at him, and kept on shaking her head until the man left her, surprised by the violence of her refusal. She saw him dancing with another girl and knew they must be talking about her, because they looked towards her and smiled.

She was trembling with the violent complexity of her feelings, of anger, hatred, jealously and bewilderment, when her husband walked up to her and pulled her affectionately by the hand.

'Get up. I'll teach you myself.'

She gripped her chair as she struggled, and the violence of her voice through clenched teeth, 'Leave me alone,' made him drop her hand with shocked surprise as the laughter left his face. She noticed his quick embarrassed glance round the room, then the hard anger of his eyes as he left her without a word. He laughed more gaily when he joined the others, to drown that moment's silence, but it enclosed her in dreary emptiness.

She had been so sure of herself in her contempt and her anger, confident of the righteousness of her beliefs, deep-based on generation-old foundations. When she had seen them being attacked, in her mind they remained indestructible, and her anger had been a sign of faith; but now she saw her husband was one of the destroyers; and yet she knew that above all others was the belief that her life must be one with his. In confusion and despair she was surrounded by ruins.

She longed for the sanctuary of the walled home from which marriage had promised an adventurous escape. Each restricting rule became a guiding stone marking a safe path through unknown dangers.

The tall woman came and sat beside her and with affection put her hand on her head.

'Tired, child?' The compassion of her voice and eyes was unbearable.

She got up and ran to the verandah, put her head against a pillar and wet it with her tears.

Ghulam Abbas

Overcoat

Translated from the Urdu

One evening in January a well-groomed young man having walked up Davis Road to the Mall turned to Charing Cross. His hair was sleek and shining and he wore sideburns. His thin moustache seemed to have been drawn with a pencil. He had on a brown overcoat with a cream coloured half-opened rose in his button hole and a green felt hat which he wore at a rakish angle. A white silk scarf was knotted at his neck. One of his hands was slipped into a pocket of his overcoat while in the other he held a short polished cane which every now and then he twirled jauntily.

It was a Saturday evening in mid-winter. The sharp icy gusts of wind struck like steel, but the young man seemed to be immune to them. So, while others were walking briskly to keep warm, he was ambling along obviously enjoying his promenade in the bitter cold.

He looked such a dandy that tonga-wallas on catching sight of him, even from a distance, whipped up their horses and raced towards him. With a wave of his stick he turned them away. A taxi also drew near him and the driver looked at him enquiringly. He too was turned off. This time with a 'No thank you.'

As he was approaching the more lively part of the Mall his spirits rose, and whistling up a 'Tango' he stepped it out as he went along. On a sudden impulse he ran a few steps and pretended to deliver a ball as if he were playing cricket.

At the turning which led to Lawrence Garden he paused for a moment as if to decide which way to go, but in the chill evening light the gardens looked sad and uninviting and so he walked straight on towards Charing Cross.

When he reached the statue of the queen he sobered down, pulled a handkerchief out of the sleeve of his overcoat where he kept it, and mopped his face.

On the lawn near the statue some English children were playing with a big rubber ball. He stopped to watch their game. At first the children did not notice him, but as he continued to stare at them they felt embarrassed and picking up their ball, laughing and shouting, chased off to the other side of the lawn. Seeing an empty cement bench by the side of the road, the young man flicked the dust off it and sat down.

As the evening advanced the cold became more intense. It was a cold that induced people to seek comfort in pleasure. At such times it was not only the profligate who ranged abroad, but even those who were usually content to live with their loneliness, emerged from their hide-outs to join in the gaiety of the streets, and to enjoy the warmth of body to body proximity. And so people converged on the Mall where they amused themselves among the variety of hotels, restaurants, cafes and snackbars, each according to his means. Those who could not afford the pleasures inside, were content to gaze at the coloured lights and brilliant advertisements outside. Up and down the main road there was an unending stream of cars, buses, tongas and bicycles while the pavements thronged with pedestrians.

The young man seated on the cement bench was watching with interest the people passing on the pavement before him. It was their clothes, rather than their faces that attracted his attention. These people belonged to all walks of life. There were traders, officials, public men, students, artists, tourists, reporters, clerks and others Most of them were wearing overcoats which were of every kind from the *astrakhan*[1] to the rough military khaki such as are found in large bundles at the secondhand clothes' shops.

The overcoat the young man himself was wearing was old, but it was well cut and the material was of good quality. The lapels were stiff and the sleeves well creased. The buttons were of horn, big and shiny. The young man seemed to be very happy in it.

A boy selling *pan*[2] and cigarettes with a tray of his wares passed by.

'Pan *Wallah*,[3]'

'Yes sir'

'Have you change for a ten *rupee* note?'

'No sir, but I'll get it for you.'

'And what if you don't come back?'

'If you don't trust me sir, you can come with me. Anyway, what do you want to buy?'

'Never mind . . . Here, I have found one *anna*. Now give me a good cigarette and be off with you.'

As he smoked he seemed to relish every puff.

A small lean white cat shivering with cold rubbed against his legs and mewed. He stroked it and it leapt up onto the bench. Smoothing its fur he muttered:

'Poor little mite.'

After a few minutes he got up.

As he was crossing the Mall the bright lights of a cinema foyer lured him. The film had already started and so there were only a few people gazing idly at the stills of future attractions displayed on the boards.

[1] a fine kind of furry wool
[2] betel leaf filled with spices, eaten after a meal
[3] man

Among these people were three young Anglo Indian girls who were giggling over a set of pictures. The young man drew towards them but as decency demanded he stood a step or two behind.

One of the girls looked back followed by nudgings and glances from the others. Suddenly she burst out laughing and the other two, trying to control themselves, pushed their companion out of the foyer. In a few seconds they were gone.

The young man seemed unconcerned at their departure and after loitering for a little while also left the cinema.

By now it was past seven. He started off again along the Mall. An orchestra could be heard playing in one of the restaurants. Many people had collected outside. Mostly they were passers-by, a few drivers of the waiting taxis and tongas,[4] labourers and beggars. Some fruit vendors having sold their fruit were also standing around with their empty baskets. These people outside seemed to be enjoying the music more than those who sat inside, for they were listening in silence though the music was foreign.

The young man also stood and listened for a moment or so, then walked on.

A few minutes later he found himself outside a large Western music shop. Without hesitation he went in. There were musical instruments of different kinds arranged on shelves around the walls. On a long table, attractively displayed, were the latest hit songs. Their cover designs were vulgar but gay. The young man cast a glance at them and then moved away towards a Spanish guitar which was hanging on the wall. He examined it with the air of a connoisseur and studied

[4] two-wheeled horse-drawn cab

the price label attached to it. Then a huge German Piano diverted his attention. Lifting the cover of the key-board he played a few notes and closed it again.

One of the salesmen came up.

'Good evening, sir,' he said courteously, 'Can I help you, sir?'

'No thank you,' the young man said with an air of indifference. Then suddenly as if remembering something he called out.

'Oh yes . . . Could you let me have a list of this month's gramophone records?'

He slipped the list into one of the pockets of his overcoat and resumed his promenade on the Mall.

He stopped next at a book stall. He picked up one or two magazines and after a hurried glance at the contents carefully replaced them. A few yards further on, a large Persian carpet, which was hanging outside a shop attracted his attention. The owner of the shop, wearing a long robe and a silk turban, greeted him warmly.

'I just wanted to see this carpet,' the young man said to the carpet dealer.

'With pleasure, sir.'

'Oh, don't bother to take it down. I can see it quite well as it is. How much is it?'

'Fourteen hundred and thirty two rupees, sir,'

The young man frowned as if to suggest, 'Oh so much.'

'You have only to select, sir,' said the carpet dealer amiably, 'and we will reduce the price to the minimum.'

'Thank you so much,' the young man said approvingly. 'A fine carpet indeed, I'll come again some time,' and he walked away.

The cream colour rose which adorned the lapel of his overcoat had slipped and was about to fall. He adjusted it with a peculiar smile of satisfaction.

He was now walking along the pavement near the High Courts. He had been roaming about for quite a long time, but his spirits were still high; he was neither tired nor bored.

At this part of the Mall the crowd of pedestrians had thinned down and there were quite long stretches of empty pavement between one group and another. The young man as he went along tried to spin his cane around one finger, but in the attempt he dropped it.

'Oh, sorry,' he exclaimed and bending down picked it up.

Meanwhile a young couple who had been walking behind him passed by and went ahead of him. The youth was tall and was wearing black corduroy trousers and a leather jacket with a zip. The girl wore a floppy *shalwar*[5] of white satin and a green coat. She was short and bulky. Her long black pigtail bobbed about her fleshy buttocks as she walked.

The young man was delighted to watch this spectacle and kept on walking behind them. They were silent for a while, then the youth said something to the girl to which she answered vehemently:

'No.'

'But as I told you the doctor is a friend of mine and no one will ever hear about it.'

'No. I said no.'

'It will be painless, and soon over.'

The girl did not reply.

'You know your parents will be terribly upset. You must think of their honour.'

'Shut up or I'll go mad.'

So far the young man had found little to interest him among the persons he had observed that evening. He

[5] baggy trousers

had been, perhaps, too deeply engrossed in himself, but there was something that fascinated him about this young couple who seemed to have stepped out of the pages of a romantic novel.

He followed them closely hoping to get a glimpse of their faces and to hear more of their talk.

By now they had reached the big cross-roads near the General Post Office. The pair stopped for a moment, then after crossing the Mall headed toward McLeod Road. The young man paused, possibly thinking that if he went after them at once they might discover that they were being followed. It would be better, perhaps, if he waited for a few moments.

When the couple had walked some hundred yards ahead of him, he hurriedly started after them. Hardly had he reached half way across the road when a truck full of bricks came from behind like a gust of wind and crushing him down speeded off towards McLeod Road. The driver of the truck had heard a shriek and had actually for a moment slowed down, but realising that something serious had happened, had taken advantage of the darkness and had sped away into the night. Two or three passers-by who had witnessed the accident shouted: 'Stop him . . . take the number,' but the truck was no more to be seen.

In a short while quite a crowd had collected. A traffic inspector on his motor bike stopped. The young man was badly hurt. There was a lot of blood about and he was in a very precarious state. A car was stopped and he was loaded into it and taken to a nearby hospital. When they reached there he was just alive.

On duty that night in the casualty department were assistant surgeon Khan and two young nurses, Shehnaz and Gill. When he was being taken to the operating theatre on a stretcher he was still wearing his brown overcoat and the silk scarf. There were large stains of blood all over his clothes. Someone had, out of sympathy, placed the young man's green felt hat on his chest so that it should not be lost.

'Seems quite well-to-do,' Nurse Shehnaz said to Nurse Gill, to which she replied in a lower tone:

'All togged up for Saturday night, poor chap.'

'Did they catch the driver?'

'No he got away.'

'What a pity!'

In the operating theatre the assistant surgeon and the two nurses with their faces concealed behind masks, were attending to the young man, only their eyes were visible. He was lying on a white marble table. His hair was still smoothed against his temples. The strong scented oil with which he had dressed it earlier that evening still gave out a faint odour.

His clothes were now being taken off. The first to be removed was the white silk scarf. Suddenly the two nurses exchanged glances. With masks on, how else could they communicate!

Beneath the scarf there was neither a tie nor a collar . . . not even a shirt. When the overcoat was removed it was found that the young man was wearing underneath only an old cotton sweater which was all in holes. Through these holes one could see the dirty vest which was in an even worse state than the sweater. The young man had wrapped the silk scarf in such a way that it hid most of his neck and chest. Layers of dirt covered his body. He could not have had a bath for at least two months. Only the upper part of his neck was clean and well powdered.

After the sweater and the vest it was the turn of the trousers to come off. Again the eyes of the two nurses met. The trousers were tightly bound at the hip with a strip of old cloth which perhaps had once been a tie. There were no buttons, no buckle. The cloth at the knees had given away, but as these parts remained under the overcoat no one could have seen them.

The shoes and the socks now came off. The shoes were old but brightly polished. As to the socks, in colour and pattern the one was quite different from the other. There were holes at the heels, and where the flesh showed through the holes it was grimed with dirt. He was by now dead and his lifeless body lay on the white marble slab.

Before his clothes were removed his face was towards the ceiling but in the process of removing his clothes it had turned towards the wall. Was it perhaps for the shame of this dual nakedness of body and soul that now he dared not face his fellow beings?

The following were the few things which were found in the various pockets of his overcoat:

A small black comb, a handkerchief, six annas and a few *pies*, a half smoked cigarette, a little diary in which the names and addresses of a few people were noted, a list of gramophone records and a few handbills which distributors had thrust upon him during his evening promenade.

Alas, his little cane, which was perhaps lost at the time of the accident, was not included in the list.

Translated by Zainab Ghulam Abbas

Suniti Namjoshi

The Blue Donkey

Inspired by a painting by Marc Chagall,
The Blue Donkey.

Once upon a time a blue donkey lived by a red bridge.
'Inartistic,' said the councillors who governed that
town. 'A donkey who lives by our bright red bridge
must be of the purest and silkiest white or we must
request that the said donkey be required to move on.'
The matter soon turned into a political issue. One party
said that donkeys never had been and never would be
white and what was asked of the donkey was grossly
unfair. If, on the other hand, the donkey were required
to be a nondescript grey (instead of a loud and laugh-
able blue), they would be prepared to accept the solution
as a reasonable way out. But the opposing party found
a fault in their logic. 'Just because donkeys have never
been known to be white,' they pointed out patiently, 'it
does not follow that a donkey is incapable of achieving
whiteness. Your argument imposes an arbitrary limita-
tion on the creature's potential.' 'Good heavens!' cried
the others. 'Are you suggesting that the donkey's blueness may be a matter of culpable wilfulness rather than
a mere genetic mischance?' Yes,' responded the
logicians. 'Let us confront the creature and you can see
for yourselves.'

They approached the donkey, who happened to be
munching a bright pink carrot which clashed most
horribly with the bright red bridge. 'O Donkey,' they
said, feeling they had better get it over with at once,
'we'd like you to turn an inoffensive grey or else move

on.' 'Can't and won't,' replied the donkey. 'There you see,' cried half the populace. 'Obviously wilful!' 'No, no,' cried the other half. 'Patently flawed!' And they began to dispute among themselves. The donkey was puzzled. 'I'm a perfectly good donkey,' she said at last. 'What exactly is the matter with you?' 'Your blueness troubles us,' wailed the citizens. 'It clashes with our bridge, as does the pinkness of your carrots. Oh what shall we do? We cannot agree among ourselves.' 'Look again,' advised the donkey. And so they did; they looked and argued and squabbled and argued and after a while most of them got used to the blueness of the donkey and didn't notice it any more. But a few remained who maintained strongly that blueness was inherent, and a few protested that it was essentially intentional. And there were still a few others who managed to see – though only sometimes – that the Blue Donkey was only herself and therefore beautiful. These last occasionally brought her a bunch of blue flowers which she put in a vase.

Saadat Hasan Manto

The Assignment

Translated from the Urdu

Beginning with isolated incidents of stabbing, it had now developed into full-scale communal violence, with no holds barred. Even home-made bombs were being used.

The general view in Amritsar was that the riots could not last long. They were seen as no more than a manifestation of temporarily inflamed political passions which were bound to cool down before long. After all, these were not the first communal riots the city had known. There had been so many of them in the past. They never lasted long. The pattern was familiar. Two weeks or so of unrest and then business as usual. On the basis of experience, therefore, the people were quite justified in believing that the current troubles would also run their course in a few days. But this did not happen. They not only continued, but grew in intensity.

Muslims living in Hindu localities began to leave for safer places, and Hindus in Muslim majority areas followed suit. However, everyone saw these adjustments as strictly temporary. The atmosphere would soon be clear of this communal madness, they told themselves.

Retired judge Mian Abdul Hai was absolutely confident that things would return to normal soon, which was why he wasn't worried. He had two children, a boy of eleven and a girl of seventeen. In addition, there was an old servant who was now pushing seventy. It was a small family. When the troubles started, Mian *sahib*,[1] being an extra cautious man, stocked up on food . . . just in case. So on one count, at least, there were no worries.

His daughter Sughra was less sure of things. They lived in a three-storey house with a view over almost the entire city. Sughra could not help noticing that whenever she went on the roof, there were fires raging everywhere. In the beginning, she could hear fire engines rushing past, their bells ringing, but this had now stopped. There were too many fires in too many places.

The nights had become particularly frightening. The sky was always lit by conflagrations like giants spitting out flames. Then there were the slogans which rent the air with terrifying frequency – Allaho Akbar, Har Har Mahadev.

Sughra never expressed her fears to her father, because he had declared confidently that there was no cause for anxiety. Everything was going to be fine. Since he was generally always right, she had initially felt reassured.

However, when the power and water supplies were suddenly cut off, she expressed her unease to her father and suggested apologetically that, for a few days at least, they should move to Sharifpura, a Muslim locality, to where many of the old residents had already moved. Mian sahib was adamant: 'You're imagining things. Everything is going to be normal very soon.'

He was wrong. Things went from bad to worse. Before long there was not a single Muslim family to be found in Mian Abdul Hai's locality. Then one day Mian sahib suffered a stroke and was laid up. His son Basharat, who used to spend most of his time playing self-devised games, now stayed glued to his father's bed.

[1] sir, master

All the shops in the area had been permanently boarded up. Dr Ghulam Hussain's dispensary had been shut for weeks and Sughra had noticed from the roof-top one day that the adjoining clinic of Dr Goranditta Mall was also closed. Mian sahib's condition was getting worse day by day. Sughra was almost at the end of her wits. One day she took Basharat aside and said to him, 'You've got to do something. I know it's not safe to go out, but we must get some help. Our father is very ill.'

The boy went, but came back almost immediately. His face was pale with fear. He had seen a blood-drenched body lying in the street and a group of wild-looking men looting shops. Sughra took the terrified boy in her arms and said a silent prayer, thanking God for his safe return. However, she could not bear her father's suffering. His left side was now completely lifeless. His speech had been impaired and he mostly communicated through gestures, all designed to reassure Sughra that soon all would be well.

It was the month of Ramadan and only two days to Id.[2] Mian sahib was quite confident that the troubles would be over by then. He was again wrong. A canopy of smoke hung over the city, with fires burning every-where. At night the silence was shattered by deafening explosions. Sughra and Basharat hadn't slept for days.

Sughra, in any case, couldn't because of her father's deteriorating condition. Helplessly, she would look at him, then at her young frightened brother and the seventy-year-old servant Akbar, who was useless for all practical purposes. He mostly kept to his bed, coughing and fighting for breath. One day Sughra told him angrily, 'What good are you? Do you realise how ill

[2] a Muslim festival

Mian sahib is? Perhaps you are too lazy to want to help, pretending that you are suffering from acute asthma. There was a time when servants used to sacrifice their lives for their masters.'

Sughra felt very bad afterwards. She had been unnecessarily harsh on the old man. In the evening when she took his food to him in his small room, he was not there. Basharat looked for him all over the house, but he was nowhere to be found. The front door was unlatched. He was gone, perhaps to get some help for Mian sahib. Sughra prayed for his return, but two days passed and he hadn't come back.

It was evening and the festival of Id was now only a day away. She remembered the excitement which used to grip the family on this occasion. She remembered standing on the roof-top, peering into the sky, looking for the Id moon and praying for the clouds to clear. But how different everything was today. The sky was covered in smoke and on distant roofs one could see people looking upwards. Were they trying to catch sight of the new moon or were they watching the fires, she wondered?

She looked up and saw the thin sliver of the moon peeping through a small patch in the sky. She raised her hands in prayer, begging God to make her father well. Basharat, however, was upset that there would be no Id this year.

The night hadn't yet fallen. Sughra had moved her father's bed out of the room onto the veranda. She was sprinkling water on the floor to make it cool. Mian sahib was lying there quietly looking with vacant eyes at the sky where she had seen the moon. Sughra came and sat next to him. He motioned her to get closer. Then he raised his right arm slowly and put it on her head. Tears began to run from Sughra's eyes. Even

Mian sahib looked moved. Then with great difficulty he said to her, 'God is merciful. All will be well.'

Suddenly there was a knock on the door. Sughra's heart began to beat violently. She looked at Basharat, whose face had turned white like a sheet of paper. There was another knock. Mian sahib gestured to Sughra to answer it. It must be old Akbar who had come back, she thought. She said to Basharat, 'Answer the door. I'm sure it's Akbar.' Her father shook his head, as if to signal disagreement.

'Then who can it be?' Sughra asked him.

Mian Abdul Hai tried to speak, but before he could do so, Basharat came running in. He was breathless. Taking Sughra aside, he whispered, 'It's a Sikh.'

Sughra screamed, 'A Sikh! What does he want?'

'He wants me to open the door.'

Sughra took Basharat in her arms and went and sat on her father's bed, looking at him desolately.

On Mian Abdul Hai's thin, lifeless lips, a faint smile appeared. 'Go and open the door. It is Gurmukh Singh.'

'No, it's someone else,' Basharat said.

Mian sahib turned to Sughra. 'Open the door. It's him.'

Sughra rose. She knew Gurmukh Singh. Her father had once done him a favour. He had been involved in a false legal suit and Mian sahib had acquitted him. That was a long time ago, but every year on the occasion of Id, he would come all the way from his village with a bag of home-made noodles. Mian sahib had told him several times, 'Sardar sahib, you really are too kind. You shouldn't inconvenience yourself every year.' But Gurmukh Singh would always reply, 'Mian sahib, God has given you everything. This is only a small gift which I bring every year in humble acknowledgement of the kindness you did me once. Even a hundred generations of mine would not be able to repay your favour. May God keep you happy.'

Sughra was reassured. Why hadn't she thought of it in the first place? But why had Basharat said it was someone else? After all, he knew Gurmukh Singh's face from his annual visit.

Sughra went to the front door. There was another knock. Her heart missed a beat. 'Who is it?' she asked in a faint voice.

Basharat whispered to her to look through a small hole in the door.

It wasn't Gurmukh Singh, who was a very old man. This was a young fellow. He knocked again. He was holding a bag in his hand, of the same kind Gurmukh Singh used to bring.

'Who are you?' she asked, a little more confident now.

'I am Sardar Gurmukh Singh's son Santokh.'

Sughra's fear had suddenly gone. 'What brings you here today?' she asked politely.

'Where is judge sahib?' he asked.

'He is not well,' Sughra answered.

'Oh, I'm sorry,' Santokh Singh said. Then he shifted his bag from one hand to the other. 'These are home-made noodles.' Then after a pause, 'Sardarji[3] is dead.'

'Dead!'

'Yes, a month ago, but one of the last things he said to me was, 'For the last ten years, on the occasion of Id, I have always taken my small gift to judge sahib. After I am gone, it will become your duty.' I gave him my word that I would not fail him. I am here today to honour the promise made to my father on his death-bed.'

---

[3] a respectful way to address a Sikh man.

Sughra was so moved that tears came to her eyes. She opened the door a little. The young man pushed the bag towards her. 'May God rest his soul,' she said.

'Is judge sahib not well?' he asked.

'No.'

'What's wrong?'

'He had a stroke.'

'Had my father been alive, it would have grieved him deeply. He never forgot judge sahib's kindness until his last breath. He used to say, "He is not a man, but a god." May God keep him under his care. Please convey my respects to him.'

He left before Sughra could make up her mind whether or not to ask him to get a doctor.

. . .

Note:
The final eight lines of this story have been removed and printed on page 186 so that you and your partners can predict them orally and in writing, and then compare the author's ending with your own.

Translated by Khalid Hasan

Manik Bandyopadhyay

The Old Woman

Translated from the Bengali

1

It is a very important day for the old woman. It is the
wedding day of her eldest great-grandson, her son's
son's son, not a small triumph for her. The home, full of
family and relatives, is humming with the busy activities
one expects on a wedding day. She is not doing anything, and they are busily going about without paying
much attention to her, the way the busy activities in a
king's palace go about without involving the king. That
is how it seems to her.

She thinks she is present, directly or indirectly, in
everything that is going on in the house on this occasion,
just as she feels she is present in all the daily activities,
the collective life of the household. For sixty years she
has been there, the roots and branches of her existence
alive with other lives so totally accustomed to her
presence that they are oblivious to it. She is like the big
old tree on the west side of the big room in the house;
its branches are full of birds busily chirping throughout
the day, and it can be heard creaking with the wind in
the dead of night.

The old woman sits in her usual corner of the porch
with her many torn quilts of rag and the bundle that
she uses as a pillow. The joints are all rusty, the spine is
bent forward, the hair flaxen, the skin loose and
wrinkled, the mouth toothless, the cheeks sunken, and

the eyes dim with cataract. Seems so very old. But when
she walks slowly with the help of a stick, one can see, if
one looks closely, that there is strength in the skin-
covered bones of her hand. When she shouts, one can
tell that there is strength in her lungs. Most of the time,
however, she spends lying down or sitting in her corner,
talking to herself. From there sometimes she criticises,
at the top of her voice, the small lapses in running the
household. She puts in her mouth ground-roasted
tobacco leaves. From time to time she breaks into her
strange sounding laughter for reasons nobody knows.

The wives of her sons and of her grandsons mutter
'There she goes again' when these strange doings make
her presence felt. The younger wives remark in low
voices. They do so not out of respect for her, because she
pretends not to hear even when she does and because it
does not matter even if they know that she hears them.
They do so for fear of offending their mothers-in-law
and the daughters of the house, who would not like big
talk in mouths that should be modest.

Nanda, the groom, has got his hair cut specially for
the occasion by Nitai the barber. Nitai has charged
eight *annas*, though he should not have because his son
was going with the groom's party as the little groom
and would get gifts. It has given the people in the house
reason to speak ill of Nitai.

The old woman calls the great-grandson to her,
'Nanda, come here. Come here, you boy with the fancy
haircut. I've a question for you. Getting ready to get
married nicely! But are you sure the girl is a virgin?'

Nanda's mother hears it and complains to her sister-
in-law, 'What an awful thing to say even as a joke!'
Then she wonders aloud, 'Maybe she has a point. She is
a grown-up girl, after all.'

'But she belongs to a good family.'

'Good families often have bad things inside. Why did they wait for so long that the girl has grown up?'

Nanda squats in front of the old woman and jokes back, 'If she is not a virgin, then she is old like you.'

She smiles a big toothless smile, 'Search the world and see if you can find a virgin like me. I hardly slept with your great-grandfather. He died on the wedding night. I was so scared to hear him breathe so hard! I was so scared that I ran out of the room crying. The people in the house came running to me, asking "What's the matter?" What's the matter, except with the writing on my forehead! By that time he was dead.'

She breaks into her cackle. But her great-grandson does not laugh. His face darkens with a cloud of doubt and suspicion. 'Maybe she is not! One is never sure of it with a grown girl!'

'Hey, you stupid monkey! How can you say such a thing? Didn't you choose her to be your wife?'

'Yes. I chose her, but . . .'

'What a stupid boy! Don't you know that a virgin can never become bad? Look at me. My husband died on the night of the wedding. As time passed, so many tried to make me become bad, but I did not. I swear by your father's head that I did not become bad. A girl goes for the bad thing only after she tastes it, not as long as she's a virgin.'

The argument may be strange, but the boy's face brightens up.

'Are you sure what you just said is true?'

'Of course, it is true.'

The people in the busy household notice Nanda squatting in front of the old woman and the two of them talking to each other in low voice; and once in a while they hear a loud cackle and a youthful laugh break out together.

2

Menaka has been weeping and lamenting all day, 'Where can I go?' I've no one to go back to!'

Nobody in the family liked Nanda's bride. Not only was she a grown girl, but also, because she had no parents and was married off by her uncle's family, they could not get back at the shrewd uncle for not giving all of the promised dowry. On top of that, Nanda had chosen her, married her against the wishes of the family, and after marriage he worshipped her without bothering about the family's feelings about it. Families never cease to be angry about the son's disobedience in marriage. Because they couldn't take it out on their earning son, their minds stayed poisoned against his wife.

On top of all of those faults of hers, Nanda died within a year of his marriage. As soon as the rainy season was over, even before the mud in the yard started drying, Nanda had started getting ready to take his wife on a trip. No wife of this family ever went on a trip alone with her husband!

Who would keep a woman with so many faults and so much ill luck?

They wrote to Menaka's uncle asking him to take her back, but the letter was not even answered. So they have decided to take Menaka to the door of her uncle's home, leave her there, and be done with it.

Menaka does not want to go. She fears not just the beatings and the burning with hot objects there, which she is used to, but she knows that her uncle would not let her in.

That is why she sits crying all day, 'Where shall I go?'

The old woman calls her to her corner of the porch,

'Hey, girl! Come over here. I have something to tell you.'

Menaka goes to her. The old woman scolds her, 'Why are you crying like a baby? A strong young woman like you?'

'Because they are throwing me out,' she says sobbing.

'Who is throwing you out? You will go merely because they want to throw you out? This is your husband's home. How can they throw you out if you refuse to leave?'

Menaka listens. The old woman goes on, 'Look at me. Could they throw me out? I spent less than one night with my husband. After he died on the wedding night, they all said, "Throw out that unlucky wife." They said that I ate my husband as soon as I got him to myself. "Out! Out!" they said. They said everything they could. Did I leave? Could anybody make me leave? I bit the ground that the home stood on and hung on. And you? You slept with your husband for almost a whole year; you lived in this house as a wife of the family. You will leave only because they want you to? Just hang on. Bite the ground this home stands on and hang on.'

Menaka's eyes light up. She squats in front of the old woman.

The family members notice Menaka and the old woman engrossed in talking, whispering to each other, about who knows what!

Translated by Kalpana Bardhan

R K Narayan

The Shelter

The rain came down suddenly. The only shelter he could run to was the big banyan tree on the roadside, with its huge trunk, and the spreading boughs above. He watched, with detachment, the rain patter down with occasional sprays coming in his direction. He watched idly a mongrel trotting off, his coat completely wet, and a couple of buffaloes on the roadside eating cast-off banana leaves. He suddenly became aware of another person standing under the tree, beyond the curve of the tree trunk. A faint scent of flowers wafted towards him, and he could not contain his curiosity. He edged along the tree trunk, and suddenly found himself face to face with her. His first reaction was to let out a loud 'Oh!', and he looked most miserable and confused. The lady saw him and suppressed a scream. When he had recovered his composure, he said, 'Don't worry, I will go away.' It seemed a silly thing to say to one's wife after a long separation. He moved back to his previous spot away from her. But presently he came back to ask, 'What brought you here?'

He feared she might not give him a reply, but she said 'Rain.' 'Oh!' He tried to treat it as a joke and tried to please her by laughing. 'It brought me also here,' he said, feeling idiotic. She said nothing in reply. The weather being an ever-obliging topic he tried to cling to it desperately and said, 'Unexpected rain.' She gave no response to his remark and looked away. He tried to drag on the subject further. 'If I had had the slightest suspicion of its coming, I would have stayed indoors or brought my umbrella.' She ignored his statement completely. She might be deaf for all it mattered. He wanted to ask, 'Are your ears affected?' but feared that she might do something desperate. She seemed capable of doing anything when she became desperate. He had never suspected the strength of her feelings until that night of final crisis.

They had several crises in their years of married life: every other hour they expressed differing views on everything under the sun: every question precipitated a crisis none too trivial to be ignored. It might be anything – whether to listen to Radio Ceylon or All-India Radio, whether one should see an English picture or a Tamil one, whether Jasmine smell might be termed too strong or otherwise, a rose could be termed gaudy or not, and so forth; anything led to an argument and created tension, and effected a breach between the partners for a number of days, to be followed by a reconciliation and an excessive friendship lasting only for a while. In one such mood of reconciliation they had even drawn an instrument of friendship with elaborate clauses, and signed it before the gods in the Puja room with a feeling that nothing would bother them again and that all their troubles were at an end, but it was short-lived and the very first clause of the contract, 'We shall never quarrel hereafter', was the first to be broken within twenty-four hours of signing the deed, and all the other clauses which covered such possible causes of difference as household expenses, criticism of food, budget discussions, references to in-laws (on all of which elaborate understanding had been evolved), did not mean anything.

Now standing in the rain he felt happy that she was cornered. He had no news of her after he had shut the door on her that night as it seemed so long ago. They had argued over the food as usual, and she threatened to leave the home, and he said, 'Go ahead,' and held the door open and she had walked out into the night. He left the door unbolted for a long time in the belief that she would return, but she didn't.

'I didn't hope to see you again,' he ventured to say now and she answered, 'Did you think I would go and drown myself?'

'Yes, that I feared,' he said.

'Did you look for me in the nearby wells, or ponds?'

'Or the river?' he added. 'I didn't.'

'It would have surprised me if you had had so much concern.'

He said, 'You didn't drown yourself after all, how could you blame me for not looking for you?' He appealed to her pathetically. She nearly stamped her foot as she said, 'That only shows you have no heart.'

'You are very unreasonable,' he said.

'Oh God, you have started giving a reading of my character. It is my ill fate that the rain should have come down just now and driven me over here.'

'On the contrary I think it is a good rain. It has brought us together. May I now ask what you have been doing with yourself all this time?'

'Should I answer?' He detected in her voice a certain amount of concern and he felt flattered. Could he induce her to come back to him? The sentence almost formed itself on the tip of his tongue but he thrust it back. He merely asked, 'Aren't you concerned with my own lot? Won't you care to know what I have been doing with myself all these months?' She didn't reply. She simply watched the rain pouring down more than ever. The wind's direction suddenly changed and a gust flung a spray of water on her face. He treated it as an excuse to dash up to her with his kerchief. She recoiled from his approach. 'Don't bother about me,' she cried.

'You are getting wet . . .' A bough above shook a few drops on her hair. He pointed his finger at her anxiously and said, 'You are getting drenched unnecessarily. You could move down a little this way. If you like I will stand where you are.' He expected her to be touched by this solitude. She merely replied, 'You need not worry about me.' She merely stood grimly looking at the rain as it churned up the road.

'Shall I dash up and bring an umbrella or a taxi?' he asked. She merely glared at him and turned away. He said something else on the same lines and she asked, 'Am I your toy?'

'Why do you say toy? I said no such thing.'

'You think you can pick me up when you like and throw me out when you feel that way. Only toys are treated thus.'

'I never told you to go away?' he said.

'I am not listening to any of that again,' she said.

'I am probably dying to say how sorry I am,' he began.

'Maybe, but go and say that to someone else.'

'I have no one else to say such things to,' he said.

'That is your trouble, is it?' she asked. 'That doesn't interest me'.

'Have you no heart?' he pleaded. 'When I say I am sorry, believe me. I am changed now.'

'So am I,' she said, 'I am not my old self now. I expect nothing in others and I am never disappointed.'

'Won't you tell me what you are doing?' he pleaded. She shook her head. He said, 'Someone said that you were doing Harijan work or some such thing. See how I am following your activities!' She said nothing in reply. He asked, 'Do you live all the time here or . . . ?' It was plain that he was trying to get her address. She threw a look at the rain, and then looked at him sourly. He said 'Well, I didn't order the rain anyway. We have got to face it together.'

'Not necessarily. Nothing can hold me thus,' she said and suddenly dashed into the rain and broke into a run. He cried after her, 'Wait, wait. I promise not to talk. Come back, don't get drenched,' but she was off, vanishing beyond the curtain of falling rain drops.

Kamala Das

Running Away from Home

When Minnie decided to run away from home to run away from her husband and the twins who were not yet one year old and the cramped apartment that always seemed to smell of wet laundry and curdled milk where the cook and the children's *ayah*[1] whispered continually like conspirators in her presence eyeing her with disdain and the thin young man who was married to her returned in the night to wake her with his cruel fidgety hands no not to talk of the day's events with her but to get it over with the lovemaking that had grown into a nightly ritual an ordeal that she bore with her eyes shut her head swimming because of the stench that emanated from his breath and his armpits it was only four in the afternoon teatime for her and milktime for the infants who had already started to whimper and from the kitchen the ayah was crying out now now it's not yet four you can't be hungry you had a heavy lunch at one farex and milk didn't you darlings and the cook in his turn shouted I can't let you have the stove now the gas is finished in the cylinder it is time for her tea she must be awake with all the hollering that has been going on here why can't you keep them quiet old women are supposed to have a way with babies you seem to be good only at spreading scandals and while the voices rose making the infants cry louder she washed her face

[1] nanny

and ran out of the house with only twenty-three rupees in her bag and a man's handkerchief slamming the door but none seemed to have heard her go walking along the road that led to the railway station she looked back twice and found the windows shut as usual the house a planet closed and self-contained and so feeling lonelier than ever before she walked on removing the rubber band in her hair letting it bounce on her shoulders with each step she took and thinking at least I have my toffee coloured hair at least I have my smile a good enough smile I am still pretty as a picture he could not destroy all of me anyway I may have turned weak I may be getting cramps on cold nights when the blanket slips off my legs but as the doctor said last week a course of vitamin b would take care of that why afterwards I would be as good as new almost as if the marriage had not taken place almost as if I were again a carefree virgin unacquainted with men's secret brutalities but of course going back to father would be unthinkable for it was he who had arranged the match coaxing her into it telling her how difficult it would be for her to complete her education her eyes being so weak after all the doctor had said so hadn't he and she had been eased out of the house no longer an eyewitness to the dalliances that went on between her father and the actress living next door who came every afternoon to use the phone with rouge on her face but she had only been fifteen then and the subject of sex had not interested her why she had been ignorant of it till the wedding night when the thin bridegroom overpowered her stabbing her vitals incessantly mercilessly so mercilessly that she had begun to sob and he asked her are you abnormal are you not a girl girls are supposed to like this and she had in desperation cried I will let you have my gold pen the parker you can also have my pocket radio you can have

anything but please stop this I cannot bear the pain but
the pain continued and the grunting that sounded
animal and when at last he slept she rose to sit on the
windowsill for the door had been locked from the
outside and there was not even a chair to sit on the
wedding gifts lying scattered all over the room on the
brass tables on the dresser and on the carpet some half
unwrapped the red tissue paper revealing the glimmer
of silver silverware gleaming blue and white in the
moonlight flowing in but she had lost interest in them
she had lost interest in the sarees of gold tissue she
herself had chosen from the best shops in Calcutta
somewhat overwhelmed by her father's sudden generosity had lost interest even in the eighteen year old boy
who had been telling her all through that summer
vacation that he was in love with her the one who sang
songs lovesongs seated with her under the asoka tree
near the pond when her grandmother was asleep and
the servants were either out or dozing in their little
rooms the one who had asked in a cracked voice when
you go back to Calcutta will you write to me will you
remember me and feeling bewildered by new emotions
she had not replied but had sat holding his warm
fingers looking on not at his pimpled face or his curly
hair but at the sun reflected in the pond and the water-
fowls young chasing their mothers going round and
round or through the henna lining water uttering their
only cry cor cor cor their yellow eyes unblinking in the
white glare of the sun and he had asked again and again
will you forget me don't you know now I love you if I
did not love you I would not have made excuses to get
here lying to my grandma about having to give you
lessons in algebra and yet you do not seem to care have
I been making a fool of myself coming here every
afternoon to sit at your feet like a slave perhaps you are

just another rich girl a spoilt city girl who would fall in
love only with a rich man somebody who owns a house
a car and a video recorder some ugly old man with
venereal diseases and she had turned round once to kiss
him lightly on his cheek knowing fully well within
herself that a kiss was no substitute for a promise – and
suddenly his eyes had turned moist making her feel
cheap yes even that boy had been forgotten after the
physical reality of the marriage dawned upon her and
the realisation that her life had been damaged even her
lifestyle changing her odour resembling his and the girl
she once had been turning into a stranger a smiling
stranger belonging to a planet of happiness with which
she could not ever again connect for she had lost all the
sunlight on the ponds the lovesongs the silence of the
afternoon and gained two children who resembled
neither herself nor the thin young man who begot them
two miniature sumo wrestlers from japan sleeping in the
large bed that had been hers before they arrived sleeping
with their vulgar ayah who snored and made guttural
sounds in her sleep lying with her saree hitched up the
flabby thighs displaying white stretchmarks the feet
displaying blackened cracks on their heels and in the
guestroom now hers and her husband's he slept heavy
against her side unwashed his nightsweat dampening
the sheets and her nightie the room slowly filling itself
with a steamy smell making her think of the bedroom
she had in her father's home the plateglass windows the
moon the mogra in bloom teddybear on the wardrobe
its left eye missing the picture on the writing table the
framed photograph of her english teacher thirty-five or
thirty-six plump and smiling a photo given on the last
day of school before the summer vacation when she had
gone into the teacher's room to bid farewell and to hand
over the poem in which she had confessed her love for

the teacher and of course the poem had made her blush
but she had said it is a marvellous poem minnie but I
cannot publish it in the school mag I hope you will
understand yes that was the season for poetry and
adoration the eighteen-year-old did not get her love
because she was already in love with her english teacher
miss laha and after the marriage when the young man
asked her if she had loved anyone she said yes I have I
have loved my english teacher miss laha and instead of
being jealous he threw back his head and laughed
revealing teeth all darkened by cigarette and iron tonics
all this she remembered as she walked towards the
railway station but no memory made her pause or regret
her decision and she bought a ticket to malad only
because the woman in front of her bought one for malad
a vegetable vendor whom she followed into the electric
train and sat on the wooden berth near her watching
the basket being shoved under the seat and the cloth
bag being pulled out from her waist the *betel*[2] and the
tobacco being taken out and chewed and then with a
sigh the woman said there is no lavatory on the trains
what are we women supposed to do when we feel the
need we can't pee through the window can we and to
establish a friendly relationship minnie smiled almost
grinned as though in appreciation of the joke and
wondered if the vendor would take her to a house where
a cook was needed or a tutor for the children for surely
she could be efficient and honest too she could make
tomato soup for the old people in the family tomato
with some cream floating on it which her father used to
like once upon a time when he had not as yet grown
cold and distant before the actress had made friends
with him during the month her mother was convalescing

[2] large leaf

in her ancestral home in the village and one day the cook had asked why don't you stop that cheap woman from coming here otherwise your father might divorce your mother to marry the slut and you will not then be able to live here like a princess with a tutor for dance a tutor for music a tutor for painting of course she had not ever spoken to the actress or even to her own father fearing his anger which she was familiar with the tempests that shook the very rafters of their house whenever she inadvertently dropped a vase in the drawing room where once every month he entertained his white friends and the brown ones who were very important so important that they almost seemed to be the white the cook wearing a starched white shirt instead of the cellular vest which he habitually wore and mother if she were in town wearing her pastels hands trembling among the tea things her mouth fumbling for words where are you going asked the vegetable vendor and minnie said I am going to malad as you can see for yourself yes said the woman but I don't recollect seeing you before on this route and suddenly the tears began to fall and in acute embarrassment minnie wiped her eyes with the large handkerchief while the woman tried to embrace her to press her weepy face to her swollen bosom smelling of cabbage whispering you are not running away from home are you I have seen girls run away from their home to become film stars and all they get is a bad reputation and maybe an illegitimate child or two the film people are rogues they will ruin you and minnie felt comforted and said no I am not thinking of joining films I was remembering my grandma she died last month and I can't get over the grief and then the woman released her grip and smiled joining films will not be a bad idea thought minnie looking out of the train after all she was not ugly she was even attractive

in a plump peachy way an artist had once called her
beautiful a bearded man who had been called to paint
grandma's portrait but when she had repeated it to her
father he had said that it only meant that the fellow
wanted her to sit for a portrait he being hard up and
needing some money yes father was being sarcastic his
usual sarcastic self she was beautiful when she dressed
as virgin mary for the passion play even the mother
superior told her so it was possible to become a film star
but it will have to be in another state and under an
assumed name for she did not want to be found out and
taken home penitent she did not want to face her father
again she did not want to face her husband either yes
she had had enough of their cruelty their sarcasm and
so she asked the vendor where is the studio that takes in
the girls who are keen on acting and the woman replied
I don't know any studio I keep myself to myself I take
vegetables to respectable people people who live in
sivaji park I don't go anywhere else why should I . . .
and then they were at malad the woman hurrying away
with her basket humming a song and minnie wading
through the crowds finding each face shuttered growing
miserable in her loneliness feeling hot and thirsty and
looking up she saw the orange spreading in the sky
above the dingy houses all in a row and each sporting
on the verandah rails an assortment of unfashionable
garments left out for drying and the road was littered
with refuse empty packets of cigarettes orange peel torn
letters and the gilded containers of contraceptives but
children were playing on the narrow pavement sometimes zigzagging through the commuters chasing rubber
balls pushing cycle tyres spinning tops with bits of dirty
string and a little girl sat on the step of her house
hugging a black kitten and all this made minnie realise
that she arrived at an unsuitable locality a transparently

poverty-stricken location where nobody was likely to feel the need for a cook or a governess and felt that she should have travelled to malabar hill or some such place but would she have known which train to take in order to reach there not having gone out much in the three years of her marriage except with her husband in his own car always too busy to give her outings being a businessman not able to relax but he once took her to the zoo at byculla showed her the fat seals heaping out of the cemented pool and three times they had been to the taj when visited the city and stayed there but even to reach the taj she would need an escort she had been forced to lead a sheltered life she was like a nun escaped from the nunnery a pathetic creature and tears streaming from the eyes she walked on and on unware of destinations feeling the eyes of men on her breasts the tired eyes of the officegoers returning to their wives and then all of a sudden she collided with a man she knew her husband's friend a lawyer used to come on sundays to play bridge with her husband and he exclaimed aloud where are you going alone what are you up to minnie and she said I have run away from home I shall not go back so don't ask me to go back I am sick and tired of my husband sick and tired of my loneliness he doesn't love me and so cannot really miss me the babies have their ayah nobody needs me there I must find myself a job you won't perhaps understand and he said I understand come with me tell me about it I can help you and he threw his arm around her walking her back to the railway station we can't possibly remain here we can go to churchgate some good restaurant in churchgate you look thirsty and she followed him into a first class compartment which was strangely empty and when the train started to move he held her cold hand in his warming it asking what kind of a job do you have in mind and she said a cook's job is okay you know I have no degree I am not qualified for any other job I could have taught english but by now I have forgotten all my grammar yes a cook's job would be the best and he laughed shaking his head no you can't possibly be a cook you don't know cooking and she cried I do I can make soups my father used to love my tomato soup and despite the ache in her heart she remembered her father with affection and the lawyer said his voice changing its timbre shedding the tenderness and turning hard no that will not do at all nobody can live on tomato soup alone face it minnie you are not qualified to do any work you are qualified only to sleep with a man yes you are a handsome wench any man would pay well to have you warm his bed you can enter a brothel there is good money in it and fun you will be able to lead a comfortable life till you are forty and then if you play your cards well you will start a brothel of your own and collect a few young girls . . . she shut her eyes tight fear tightening itself into a knot within her bosom hands turning cold and she said weakly no that cannot be I would rather die than be one of those women and felt suddenly a sloppy kiss on her face near her mouth the saliva the spittle lingering on her skin like a postal stamp and felt his rough hands groping within her blouse and the contours of his body crushing her limbs and pushing him away breathless she cried I want to go home I want to see my husband I want my children please take me home . . .

Rabindranath Tagore

The Babus of Nayanjore

Translated from the Bengali

1

Once upon a time the Babus of Nayanjore were famous landholders. They were noted for their princely extravagance. They would tear off the rough border of their Dacca muslin, because it rubbed against their skin. They could spend many thousands of rupees over the wedding of a kitten. On a certain grand occasion it is alleged that in order to turn night into day they lighted numberless lamps and showered silver threads from the sky to imitate sunlight. Those were the days before the flood. The flood came. The line of succession among these old-world Babus, with their lordly habits, could not continue for long. Like a lamp with too many wicks burning, the oil flared away quickly, and the light went out.

Kailas Babu, our neighbour, is the last relic of this extinct magnificence. Before he grew up, his family had very nearly reached its lowest ebb. When his father died, there was one dazzling outburst of funeral extravagance, and then insolvency. The property was sold to liquidate the debt. What little ready money was left over was altogether insufficient to keep up the past ancestral splendours.

Kailas Babu left Nayanjore and came to Calcutta. His son did not remain long in this world of faded glory. He died, leaving behind him an only daughter.

In Calcutta we are Kailas Babu's neighbours. Curiously enough our own family history is just the opposite to his. My father got his money by his own exertions, and prided himself on never spending a penny more than was needed. His clothes were those of a working man, and his hands also. He never had any inclination to earn the title of Babu by extravagant display, and I myself, his only son, owe him gratitude for that. He gave me the very best education, and I was able to make my way in the world. I am not ashamed of the fact that I am a self-made man. Crisp banknotes in my safe are dearer to me than a long pedigree in an empty family chest.

I believe this was why I disliked seeing Kailas Babu drawing his heavy cheques on the public credit from the bankrupt bank of his ancient Babu reputation. I used to fancy that he looked down on me, because my father had earned money with his own hands.

I ought to have noticed that no one showed any vexation towards Kailas Babu except myself. Indeed it would have been difficult to find an old man who did less harm than he. He was always ready with his kindly little acts of courtesy in times of sorrow and joy. He would join in all the ceremonies and religious observances of his neighbours. His familiar smile would greet young and old alike. His politeness in asking details about domestic affairs was untiring. The friends who met him in the street were perforce ready to be button-holed, while a long string of questions of this kind followed one another from his lips:

'My dear friend, I am delighted to see you. Are you quite well? How is Shashi? and Dada – is he all right? Do you know, I've only just heard that Madhu's son has got fever. How is he? Have you heard? And Hari Charan Babu – I have not seen him for a long time – I hope he is not ill. What's the matter with Rakkhal? And, er – er, how are the ladies of your family?'

Kailas Babu was spotlessly neat in his dress on all occasions, though his supply of clothes was sorely limited. Every day he used to air his shirts and vests and coats and trousers carefully, and put them out in the sun, along with his bed-quilt, his pillow-case, and the small carpet on which he always sat. After airing them he would shake them, and brush them, and put them on the rock. His little bits of furniture made his small room decent, and hinted that there was more in reserve if needed. Very often, for want of a servant, he would shut up his house for a while . Then he would iron out his shirts and linen with his own hands, and do other little menial tasks. After this he would open his door and receive his friends again.

Though Kailas Babu, as I have said, had lost all his landed property, he had still some family heirlooms left. There was a silver cruet for sprinkling scented water, a filigree box for otto-of-roses, a small gold salver, a costly ancient shawl, and the old-fashioned ceremonial dress and ancestral turban. These he had rescued with the greatest difficulty from the money-lenders' clutches. On every suitable occasion he would bring them out in state, and thus try to save the world-famed dignity of the Babus of Nayanjore. At heart the most modest of men, in his daily speech he regarded it as a sacred duty, owed to his rank, to give free play to his family pride. His friends would encourage this trait in his character with kindly good-humour, and it gave them great amusement.

The neighbourhood soon learnt to call him their *Thakur Dada*.[1] They would flock to his house, and sit

[1] Grandfather

with him for hours together. To prevent his incurring any expense, one or other of his friends would bring him tobacco, and say: 'Thakur Dada, this morning some tobacco was sent to me from Gaya. Do take it, and see how you like it.'

Thakur Dada would take it, and say it was excellent. He would then go on to tell of a certain exquisite tobacco which they once smoked in the old days at Nayanjore at the cost of a guinea an ounce.

'I wonder,' he used to say, 'I wonder if anyone would like to try it now. I have some left, and can get it at once.'

Everyone knew that, if they asked for it, then somehow or other the key of the cupboard would be missing; or else Ganesh, his old family servant, had put it away somewhere.

'You never can be sure,' he would add, 'where things go to when servants are about. Now, this Ganesh of mine – I can't tell you what a fool he is, but I haven't the heart to dismiss him.'

Ganesh, for the credit of the family, was quite ready to bear all the blame without a word.

One of the company usually said at this point: 'Never mind, Thakur Dada. Please don't trouble to look for it. This tobacco we're smoking will do quite well. The other would be too strong.'

Then Thakur Dada would be relieved, and settle down again, and the talk would go on.

When his guests got up to go away, Thakur Dada would accompany them to the door, and say to them on the doorstep: 'Oh, by the way, when are you all coming to dine with me?'

One or other of us would answer: 'Not just yet, Thakur Dada, not just yet. We'll fix a day later.'

'Quite right,' he would answer. 'Quite right. We had

much better wait till the rains come. It's too hot now. And a grand rich dinner such as I should want to give you would upset us in weather like this.'

But when the rains did come, everyone was very careful not to remind him of his promise. If the subject was brought up, some friend would suggest gently that it was very inconvenient to get about when the rains were so severe, that it would be much better to wait till they were over. And so the game went on.

His poor lodging was much too small for his position, and we used to condole with him about it. His friends would assure him they quite understood his difficulties: it was next to impossible to get a decent house in Calcutta. Indeed, they had all been looking out for years for a house to suit him, but, I need hardly add, no friend had been foolish enough to find one. Thakur Dada used to say, after a long sigh of resignation: 'Well, well, I suppose I shall have to put up with this house after all.' Then he would add with a genial smile: 'But, you know, I could never bear to be away from my friends. I must be near you. That really compensates for everything.'

Somehow I felt all this very deeply indeed. I suppose the real reason was, that when a man is young stupidity appears to him the worst of crimes. Kailas Babu was not really stupid. In ordinary business matters everyone was ready to consult him. But with regard to Nayanjore his utterances were certainly void of common sense. Because, out of amused affection for him, no one contradicted his impossible statements, he refused to keep them in bounds. When people recounted in his hearing the glorious history of Nayanjore with absurd exaggerations he would accept all they said with the utmost gravity, and never doubted, even in his dreams, that anyone could disbelieve it.

2

When I sit down and try to analyse the thoughts and feelings that I had towards Kailas Babu, I see that there was a still deeper reason for my dislike. I will now explain.

Though I am the son of a rich man, and might have wasted time at college, my industry was such that I took my MA degree in Calcutta University when quite young. My moral character was flawless. In addition, my outward appearance was so handsome, that if I were to call myself beautiful, it might be thought a mark of self-estimation, but could not be considered an untruth.

There could be no question that among the young men of Bengal I was regarded by parents generally as a very eligible match. I was myself quite clear on the point, and had determined to obtain my full value in the marriage market. When I pictured my choice, I had before my mind's eye a wealthy father's only daughter, extremely beautiful and highly educated. Proposals came pouring in to me from far and near; large sums in cash were offered. I weighed these offers with rigid impartiality, in the delicate scales of my own estimation. But there was no one fit to be my partner. I became convinced, with the poet Bhabavuti, that

In this world's endless time and boundless space
One may be born at last to match my sovereign
    grace.

But in this puny modern age, and this contracted space of modern Bengal, it was doubtful if the peerless creature existed as yet.

Meanwhile my praises were sung in many tunes, and in different metres, by designing parents.

Whether I was pleased with their daughters or not, this worship which they offered was never unpleasing. I used to regard it as my proper due, because I was so good. We are told that when the gods withold their boons from mortals they still expect their worshippers to pay them fervent honour, and are angry if it is withheld. I had that divine expectance strongly developed in myself.

I have already mentioned that Thakur Dada had an only grand-daughter. I had seen her many times, but had never mistaken her for beautiful. No thought had ever entered my mind that she would be a possible partner for myself. All the same, it seemed quite certain to me that some day or other Kailas Babu would offer her, with all due worship, as an oblation at my shrine. Indeed – this was the secret of my dislike – I was thoroughly annoyed that he had not done it already.

I heard he had told his friends that the Babus of Nayanjore never craved a boon. Even if the girl remained unmarried, he would not break the family tradition. It was this arrogance of his that made me angry. My indignation smouldered for some time. But I remained perfectly silent, and bore it with the utmost patience, because I was so good.

As lightning accompanies thunder, so in my character a flash of humour was mingled with the mutterings of my wrath. It was, of course, impossible for me to punish the old man merely to give vent to my rage; and for a long time I did nothing at all. But suddenly one day such an amusing plan came into my head, that I could not resist the temptation of carrying it into effect.

I have already said that many of Kailas Babu's friends used to flatter the old man's vanity to the full. One, who was a retired Government servant, had told him that whenever he saw the Chota Lord Sahib he always asked for the latest news about the Babus of Nayanjore, and the Chota Lord had been heard to say that in all Bengal the only really respectable families were those of the Maharaja of Burdwan and the Babus of Nayanjore. When this monstrous falsehood was told to Kailas Babu he was extremely gratified, and often repeated the story. And wherever after that he met this Government servant in company he would ask, along with other questions:

'Oh! er – by the way, how is the Chota Lord Sahib? Quite well, did you say? Ah, yes, I am so delighted to hear it! And the dear Mem Sahib, is she quite well too? Ah, yes! and the little children – are they quite well also? Ah, yes! that's very good news! Be sure and give them my compliments when you see them.'

Kailas Babu would constantly express his intention on going some day and paying a visit to the Sahib. But it may be taken for granted that many Chota Lords and Burra Lords also would come and go, and much water would pass down the Hooghly, before the family coach of Nayanjore would be furnished up to pay a visit to Government House.

One day I took Kailas Babu aside, and told him in a whisper: 'Thakur Dada, I was at the Levee yesterday, and the Chota Lord happened to mention the Babus of Nayanjore. I told him that Kailas Babu had come to town. Do you know, he was terribly hurt because you hadn't called. He told me he was going to put etiquette on one side, and pay you a private visit himself this very afternoon.'

Anybody else could have seen through this plot of mine in a moment. And, if it had been directed against another person, Kailas Babu would have understood the joke. But after all he had heard from his friend the Government servant, and after all his own exaggerations, a visit from the Lieutenant-Governor seemed the most natural thing in the world. He became highly nervous and excited at my news. Each detail of the coming visit exercised him greatly – most of all his own ignorance of English. How on earth was that difficulty to be met? I told him there was no difficulty at all: it was aristocratic not to know English: and, besides, the Lieutenant-Governor always brought an interpreter with him, and he had expressly mentioned that this visit was to be private.

About midday, when most of our neighbours are at work, and the rest are asleep, a carriage and pair stopped before the lodging of Kailas Babu. Two flunkeys in livery came up the stairs, and announced in a loud voice, 'The Chota Lord Sahib has arrived.' Kailas Babu was ready, waiting for him, in his old-fashioned cere-monial robes and ancestral turban, and Ganesh was by his side, dressed in his master's best suit of clothes for the occasion. When the Chota Lord Sahib was announced, Kailas Babu ran panting and puffing and trembling to the door, and led in a friend of mine, in disguise, with repeated salaams, bowing low at each step, and walking backward as best he could. He had his old family shawl spread over a hard wooden chair, and he asked the Lord Sahib to be seated. He then made a high-flown speech in Urdu, the ancient Court language of the Sahibs, and presented on the golden salver a string of gold *mohurs*,[2] the last relics of his broken fortune. The old family servant Ganesh, with an expression of awe bordering on terror, stood behind with the scent-sprinkler, drenching the Lord Sahib, touching him gingerly from time to time with the otto-of-roses from the filigree box.

[2] a former gold coin of India and Persia

Kailas Babu repeatedly expressed his regret at not being able to receive His Honour Bahadur with all the ancestral magnificence of his own family estate at Nayanjore. There he could have welcomed him properly with due ceremonial. But in Calcutta he was a mere stranger and sojourner – in fact a fish out of water.

My friend, with his tall silk hat on, very gravely nodded. I need hardly say that according to English custom the hat ought to have been removed inside the room. But my friend did not dare to take it off for fear of detection; and Kailas Babu and his old servant Ganesh were sublimely unconscious of the breach of etiquette.

After a ten minutes' interview, which consisted chiefly of nodding the head, my friend rose to his feet to depart. The two flunkeys in livery, as had been planned beforehand, carried off in state the string of gold mohurs, the gold salver, the old ancestral shawl, the silver scent-sprinkler, and the otto-of-roses filigree box; they placed them ceremoniously in the carriage. Kailas Babu regarded this as the usual habit of Chota Lord Sahibs.

I was watching all the while from the next room. My sides were aching with suppressed laughter. When I could hold myself in no longer, I rushed into a further room, suddenly to discover, in a corner, a young girl sobbing as if her heart would break. When she saw my uproarious laughter she stood upright in passion, flashing the lightning of her big dark eyes in mine, and said with a tear-choked voice: 'Tell me! What harm has my grandfather done to you? Why have you come to deceive him? Why have you come here? Why – '

She could say no more. She covered her face with her hands, and broke into sobs.

My laughter vanished in a moment. It had never occurred to me that there was anything but a supremely funny joke in this act of mine, and here I discovered that I had given the cruellest pain to this tenderest little heart. All the ugliness of my cruelty rose up to condemn me. I slunk out of the room in silence, like a kicked dog.

Hitherto I had only looked upon Kusum, the grand-daughter of Kailas Babu, as a somewhat worthless commodity in the marriage market, waiting in vain to attract a husband. But now I found, with a shock of surprise, that in the corner of that room a human heart was beating.

The whole night through I had very little sleep. My mind was in a tumult. On the next day, very early in the morning, I took all those stolen goods back to Kailas Babu's lodgings, wishing to hand them over in secret to the servant Ganesh. I waited outside the door, and, not finding any one, went upstairs to Kailas Babu's room. I heard from the passage Kusum asking her grandfather in the most winning voice: 'Dada, dearest, do tell me all that the Chota Lord Sahib said to you yesterday. Don't leave out a single word. I am dying to hear it all over again.'

And Dada needed no encouragement. His face beamed over with pride as he related all manner of praises which the Lord Sahib had been good enough to utter concerning the ancient families of Nayanjore. The girl was seated before him, looking up into his face, and listening with rapt attention. She was determined, out of love for the old man, to play her part to the full.

My heart was deeply touched, and tears came to my eyes. I stood there in silence in the passage, while Thakur Dada finished all his embellishments of the Chota Lord Sahib's wonderful visit. When he left the room at last, I took the stolen goods and laid them at the feet of the girl and came away without a word.

Later in the day I called again to see Kailas Babu himself. According to our ugly modern custom, I had been in the habit of making no greeting at all to this old man when I came into the room. But on this day I made a low bow, and touched his feet. I am convinced the old man thought that the coming of the Chota Lord Sahib to his house was the cause of my new politeness. He was highly gratified by it, and an air of benign severity shone from his eyes. His friends had flocked in, and he had already begun to tell again at full length the story of the Lieutenant-Governor's visit with still further adornments of a most fantastic kind. The interview was already becoming an epic, both in quality and in length.

When the other visitors had taken their leave, I made my proposal to the old man in a humble manner. I told him that though I could never for a moment hope to be worthy of marriage connection with such an illustrious family, yet . . . etc. etc.

When I made clear my proposal of marriage, the old man embraced me, and broke out in a tumult of joy: 'I am a poor man, and could never have expected such great good fortune.'

That was the first and last time in his life that Kailas Babu confessed to being poor. It was also the first and last time in his life that he forgot, if only for a single moment, the ancestral dignity that belongs to the Babus of Nayanjore.

Translated by C F Andrews with the Author's help.

Shaukat Osman

Charity

Translated from the Bengali

1

Kalam Majumdar had made a lot of money by various means. During the last twenty years he had not known defeat in the realm of business. He had the golden touch. Now his property was valued at over ten millions.

A successful man may have endless whims born of security. Possibly for some such reason or other – there is hardly any point in trying to locate the source – Kalam Majumdar had a whim, yes whim it must be, that he wanted to become a beggar. He would give away all his property and recast his life. He who had never known defeat, was suddenly gripped by his excitement: he would gamble it all away. Destiny had often smiled at him at flash boards. Even the first capital for his business was won at a gambling table. He would gamble again. Indeed, it was too big a gamble, not far from insanity.

One morning Majumdar declared to his friends that he would give away all his property. He could realise at least ten millions if he sold his property. He would give it all away to the poor.

Many thought it was one of Majumdar's stunts. It was inconceivable that one who lived like a king would wilfully become a beggar.

Many did not believe him even when he declared his intention in the press. The emergence of a *Haji*

Mohsin[1] in this age could be given no more credence than that given to a fairy tale.

But there was no room for scepticism when Majumdar declared the place, date and conditions of his projected charity. Not only that; he even started selling his business and factories. It was at this stage that his friend Tarek Mirza came to warn him.

Majumdar had not lied. His project made due progress. He wouldn't listen to anyone. What could you do if one was bent upon destroying oneself?

2

'I, Kalam Majumdar, son of Bakhtiar Majumdar, village Gourgram, district . . . do hereby declare that I shall give away the whole of my earned property, the value of which is more or less ten million *rupees*[2], on the first day of Vaishakha[3], . . . to the poor who present themselves on the said date.

'This charity will begin at sunrise and will proceed until sunset after which nothing will be given away.

'It should also be noted that certain arrangements have been made for the convenience of the needy.

'The charity will take place at the open field, covering an area of six miles, in front of my village home. The following arrangements have been made to facilitate the charity work:

1 Coins have been placed in separate enclosures of strong wooden fencing. First there will be new *paisas*[4]

---

[1] Muslim person who has made a pilgrimage
[2] a coin worth about 5 pence
[3] name of a month in the Hindu Calendar
[4] 100 paisas = 1 rupee

only, then in the next enclosure two paisas; then five paisas, ten paisas. In the same manner, quarter and half rupee coins, one, five and ten rupee notes will be placed in separate enclosures in the above order.

2 It should be remembered that as it is not possible to hand out so much money, coins and notes will be laid out on tables within the aforementioned enclosures. Everyone will take a paisa and then move on to the next enclosure. There is no rule against leaping over the fences.

3 Only one thousand rupee notes may be taken from me and my associates after the last fence has been crossed.

4 It should be remembered in this connexion that there is only one entrance. Everyone will enter through the gate for new paisas. This will lead to other gates.

5 I appeal most humbly to my compatriots to help me in completing the job with order and discipline. My poor compatriots are the real owners of the money earned in the country. I want to repay my debts by returning the money to those to whom it should belong. I hope, brothers and sisters, you will be kind to me.'

The above declaration began to be published in all the newspapers as an advertisement. Not for a day or two but over a few weeks. Many had originally thought that the whole thing was a hoax. Now there was no room for such scepticism. Many newspapermen searched him out after the advertisements started coming out. Editorials were published on his great endeavour. The whole country seethed with excitement at this strange declaration.

3

All reads lead to Rome. Now all roads of the country led to Gourgram. It was a fortnight to the first of Vaishakha. But there was already an uproar in the district. Where would you find an easier way to obtain money. You could start life again if you could get hold of a thousand rupee note. The beggars thought: even fifty was not bad. Not only beggars, many unemployed once again found a chance to grapple with life. Thieves and robbers thought, here was a God given chance. Those who earned their honest penny but found it difficult to make both ends meet, thought if God wanted to give them some windfall there was no harm in taking it. Where could one find such money without having to work for it? God willing, one's destiny could take a turn. Even some respectable people gave way after having fought an unequal battle with their conscience. Young men who sought excitement at every step thought it wasn't bad even if they could grab enough for a cinema ticket. The whole country turned its eyes towards Gourgram.

The beggars of far away Rangpur and Dinajpur districts thought it was better to start now. Those who had saved a little boarded trains. Not only to this class of people but to all, solution to their problems came in the form of one slogan: Onward to Gourgram! As a result it was difficult to get room on the trains. There were accidents at several places. People had fallen off the roofs of trains. River-routes were in a similar situation. Everyone wanted to be there. The vessels were naturally over-crowded. There was news of boats capsizing at two different places. More heart-rending perhaps was the news of a motor boat capsizing. Two or three hundred people vanished to the bottom of the river. The poor *serang*[5] got beaten up by the mob, although it was the passengers themselves who in their eagerness to reach the charity ground had persuaded him to accommodate them in his overcrowded boat. If they did not arrive a day or two earlier, there was no guarantee that they would even approach the gate. So everybody was bent upon making the best use of their time. And that was the trouble.

The village was fast becoming a holy place. Everyday various news and all kinds of information relating to Gourgram appeared in the newspapers. An enthusiastic reporter even published a map with his report. This is how an obscure village hit the headlines.

'Ask traveller about his destination, he will reply, "Gourgram," but he won't disclose his intention. Ask him why and he will say, "to see the fun."

Let's now take a look at the arrangements for the charity project.

It was really a vast field looking deserted now that harvesting was over. Apart from the trace of the next village far away, void seemed to be more natural here.

Majumdar had left no lacuna in his arrangements. Four or five miles of field was surrounded by barbed wire. The wooden fences were inside this area. Strong *shal*[6] trunks were used for pillars; and varieties of thick wooden staves were used to make the fences. A couple of hundred or a thousand people wouldn't be able to smash them down. The fences were ten feet high: it was quite difficult to leap over them. But then one could put

[5] boatman
[6] a kind of tree

ones toes in the crannies and try to climb over. Money was laid out as advertised. Majumdar had mustered a massive supply of coins. It's surprising how the banks had supplied that amount.

However, there was one obvious difficulty. Say, one took his share of paisas and wanted naturally to rush towards quarter, half or one rupee counters. To do so he would have to come out and re-enter through the gates for quarter, half and one rupee enclosures. But no one would care to spoil so much time. Every one would try to leap over the fences. The lame would find it particularly difficult.

Majumdar's own seat was at the very end of the line. A fifty-feet wide wooden dais had been constructed. There were some chairs on it and a table in front of them. Money had not yet arrived. Majumdar would fetch it on the day of charity. There was the fear of thieves and robbers. Majumdar had already brought a hundred or so policemen. After the act of charity, however, he would no longer need any guards for himself. He would join the ranks of those to whom he was now going to give away his wealth.

A lot of money had been spent in making these arrangements. Even barbed wire cost a great deal not to speak of wood and nails.

A few shops had sprung up around the place such as *pan*[7] shops and tea stalls. Crowds had started converging to the area for about a week now.

Armed policemen were to be posted at the gates to the enclosures. So a few tents had been pitched.

Gourgram had not seen such fanfare in a thousand years. Majumdar himself visited his village once in a blue moon: the city was his centre of activities. Heaven

[7] betel leaf filled with spices

knows why he felt this sudden urge to return to the land of his forefathers. The arrangements could be described in a word as excellent.

Indeed one could not hold Majumdar responsible for the accidents which took place on the river routes or railroads.

The first of Vaisakha was imminent. Only a few days were to go.

In the late afternoon of the last day of Chaitra[8] one could see nothing but human heads. There was a lot of pushing and shoving at the gate already. The gates would be thrown open in the morning of the next day. As everyone wanted to be in the first row, there was more noise near the gate.

It was difficult even to move around. People were packed like sardines.

And wherever there was a crowd of this size, problems were bound to crop up. Many beggars had leprosy; they too wanted to make room for themselves in the crowd. How long would you expect them to avoid physical contact? Besides, here everyone was a beggar: everyone had the same rights. One couldn't be choosy. Those who did not want to take much risk fell back. However, there was a lot of money here and one hoped to have a share in it. With such hope, however one was jostled by the crowd, one could not leave one's place and go away in vexation. They all stayed on suppressing their personal grievances. Those who had strength in their elbows of course gave a nudge or two to those nearest to them.

It was difficult to give an exact description of the crowd: there were so many types of people. All of them, however, had a psychological affinity on one point which

---

[8] name of a month in the Hindu Calendar

could be generally expressed as: Let's have something, for Heaven's sake. Detailed study of faces or of psychology was beyond anyone's power.

Various types of people: various dialects. How could you expect the beggar from Bogra to understand the beggar from Chittagong? Yet this difference helped. If the man from Noakhali dug his elbow into the side of a Dinajpuri weakling, the latter could then seek the help of his regional brother to give the brute a suitable answer. In this sea of men the currents moved so fast and so unpredictably that it was impossible to give an exact account of what was happening.

4

With sunrise the dam that somehow stood the flood gave in. Uncontrollable masses of people rushed through the gate and immediately all discipline vanished. The first gate led to the enclosure for paisas. But who would care to go there? Moreover, they were new paisas. So attempts at climbing over the fences started immediately. But that was not easy. Everyone wanted to go ahead of others. As a result, some fell on their faces at the foot of the fence, fell, that is, never to get up. They screamed but who would listen? Here everyone was for himself. Everyone was egoistic.

There was a stampede outside the gate. It looked as if a few hundred crocodiles were pursuing their prey on a deserted islet in the Padma, beating their tails. Those who were weaker, or had become so in their effort to go in, had already fallen on their faces. Their heads and torso as well as their screams were being crushed under innumerable feet.

If someone started climbing a fence, his contender

went and held him by his leg. The poor man, now swung back, would then take it up with the offender, and a fight would start. And the earth would no longer remain dry. Blood, which was known to have always soaked the earth of this country, replaced dew and rain. Only those who had necessary strength and whose ears were sealed to painful cries around could still move ahead in a mad rush.

But it was not easy to move on. One had to take something. Otherwise, what was the point of coming here? So one had to grab before others. But there were no less than two hundred thousand hands – all hungry, ravening like tongues of cannibals. If a hand was extended, it struck against other hands, struck hard, and then you had to strike back.

Everybody looked ahead. What was the use of wasting time on quarter and half rupee coins? Some were more ambitious . . . Let's go towards the gate for fivers. A few thousand had already swarmed there. But the scene at the table was similar to the scene at the fences. Who would listen to the rules of charity? Take as much you can! If you had one hundred notes, you had five hundred rupees. So hands were no longer hands: they had become paws. Claws. Paws struggled with paws. If someone pawed about ten notes, ten others swung their paws and grabbed the notes by the other end. The tug of war ended with fifty rupees torn to pieces in a moment. Then the inevitable obscenities. They called one another's mothers tarts and then fought like gallant sons. You had supporters to egg you on. The supporters of one group were matched by those of the other. Men formed into groups and riots started. Meanwhile the bank notes, now torn to shreds, were trodden under their feet.

The fair wind of charity had transformed the wide

open field of Gourgram into a wild jungle. The stream of men had to find their identity in a stream of blood.

Some of them would love to get out of the place with their lives but that was not easy. There were barbed wire fences all around the place and there was only one exit – the paisa gate. It was difficult to return because you had to force your way through an equally packed crowd. It was even difficult because you lacked the incentive that had goaded you on your way in. So you had no other alternative but to let yourself go with the crowd.

Even the idea of returning was difficult for many. Mymoon Bibi of Dinajpur had spent all her savings and suffered many a trial having travelled by rail, steamer, and on foot. Her physical strength encouraged her. Her son too was a strong young man. And with them was the pre-adolescent son of Mymoon Bibi's widowed daughter. As he was a fatherless child his grandmother couldn't bring herself to leave him behind. Now old Mymoon had none of her companions with her. With her own eyes she had seen her grandson being trampled under innumerable feet; she had not been able to protect him. She had seen her son fighting for a ten rupee note. Then he was borne away by the crowd. Overhead the Vaisakha sky had now lit with the fire of hell. Exhausted by sweat and desperate remorse Mymoon Bibi had no strength left in her. She somehow stood by a fence to cry by herself, to stifle her remorse.

Look in that direction! A man wanted to climb over the fence between the five rupee enclosure and the ten rupee enclosure. He was injured, bleeding. Still he must go on. He was not yet beaten. He grabbed three five rupee notes. If he could get over the fence, his destiny might smile. One of his feet ached. No matter. He tried two or three times without success. A sentry was there.

The man appealed to the sentry without result. He pulled out one of his five rupee notes and then secured the assistance of the sentry who agreed to push him over the fence. But it cost him a little more: he had to part with one more of his notes. The man, however, had no remorse. He would make it up if he could grab even one note on the other side of the fence.

You could see Majumdar's dais five miles away. He sat there watching everything. He had sufficiently advertised the rules in the papers. If they wouldn't abide by the rules, what could he do?

There was no recess in the uproar. Nobody had yet been able to enter the hundred rupee note enclosure because pushing and shoving, fighting, swearing, shouting and crying continued unabated. And nobody listened to anybody.

The heat of the sun was more unbearable than usual. Nobody had eaten or drunk as they would normally do. One needed energy and strength to obtain what was there to obtain over the length and breadth of the area of five miles. How many had the strength?

About noontide a man was seen collapsing against a fence. He had a few quarter and half rupee coins in his fist. Another man while running past him, snatched those coins away. The body lay where it had fallen. Many alike had collapsed out of thirst. Some took to the ground for eternal rest from loss of blood.

The rhythm here was now low, now high, but there was always a rhythm. Greed, blood thirst, revengefulness ruled in all their savagery.

Mymoon Bibi looked about for her son. He was found hanging from barbed wire. The unfortunate man had apparently given up hope and had tried to go out over the barbed wire fence. The barbed wire had not forgiven him. To beg and yet not follow rules, hadn't worked.

Mymoon Bibi did not cry, she just laughed. During quieter moments her laughter could be heard from far away. For a long time.

The sun set and the charity stopped. Only a few had got into the hundred rupee enclosure. Here one could only take one note each. They had left with that. You could break rules in the crowd but it was not possible to do so here.

The bulk of Majumdar's money was saved. Mymoon Bibi went around the field laughing and crying, repeating over and over again: 'Oh God, how shall I ever go back to Dinajpur?'[9]

She showed a coin and laughed; 'This won't cover the rail fare to Dinajpur, will it?'

Translated by Osman Jamal

[9] Dinajpur is 300 kilometres away.

Gulabhdas Broker

And Now She's Dead

Translated from the Gujarati by the author

Startled at the touch of a hand on my shoulder, I swung around. A huge Sikh, tall and strong, with an embarrassed expression on his face, was standing just behind me.

'Please forgive me, *Huzur*,'[1] he muttered, as our eyes met.

The moment I saw him my fear vanished. Otherwise, to be accosted by a stranger in that manner at that late hour on the deserted roads of this small hill-station of Lonavala was an experience likely to give shivers even to the bravest of hearts.

'It is all right, brother,' I said with a smile, 'but what is it you want?'

'Nothing – nothing, please. Only I-er-I-', he hesitated a moment. Then, in a voice shy yet bold, he asked:

'Will you forgive me, please, if I ask you if you know English?'

I laughed. "Oh, hm, yes, a little. Why?'

'I was sure you knew it,' he beamed. 'When you were looking at that envelope in your hand under the light of the street-lamp, I could see that the writing on it was in English. And therefore I dared to bother the Huzur.'

'How are you concerned with my knowledge of English, and that too at this late hour?' I asked.

[1] a respectful way to address one's superior

120

'If the Huzur does not mind, I should like him to read for me a letter in English.'

'When?'

'Whenever the Huzur pleases,' he replied politely, but his whole face was like an open book, with only one sentence written on it. I could interpret that sentence very clearly. 'Read it immediately,' he begged.

'What is it about?' I countered.

'How should I know it without knowing English? That is why I want the Huzur's help,' he laughed.

I felt curious. What could it be about?

'You want me to read it just now?'

'Will it not be very inconvenient just now?' he said diffidently, but I could see joy light up his face at the mere thought of the contents of the letter being disclosed to him without delay.

'I am going to the Post Office to post this letter. Shall we read your letter there?' I suggested.

'Thanks, many many thanks, Huzur,' was his fervent reply, and we moved on.

Those two furlongs to the Post Office were covered in silence. He was deep in his own thoughts and I was wondering what it could all be about. It could have nothing to do with a job or some such thing, surely, because in that case he could certainly have given a clear answer to my question. But if it was not that, what else could it be? Certainly no romance could be involved in it, because then the epistle would have been written in a language this man could read and understand. But if there were not something intimate about the whole business, to what then were due his shyness, his embarrassment, his irrepressible desire to know the contents of the letter as soon as he possibly could?

On reaching the Post Office I pointed to a bench outside and said:

'Shall we sit down here?'

'There will not be much light here, *Janab*.[2] Should we not, rather, go and sit in the restaurant opposite?'

I posted my letter and followed him across the road. We sat at a table with a light over it. I stretched out my hand and asked for the letter. He again felt shy and embarrassed as he handed it to me.

'I am giving you a lot of trouble, Huzur.'

'No, no, it is nothing, my dear man,' I said, taking the letter from him.

As I read the contents my eyes often roamed over his face. He, in his turn, was gazing at me with a fixed and eager stare.

I finished reading his letter and smiled at him.

'What does it say, Janab?' he asked anxiously.

'Are you Kartar Singh?'

'Yes, please.'

'All this correspondence is about yourself?'

In a small voice he replied, 'Yes, yes.'

'So you want to marry, eh?'

'Do they write to say that it is possible?' He got up, excited.

'Sit down, *Sardarji*,[3] please sit down,' I chuckled. 'Even if they wrote to say yes, there is no train leaving just now. So do sit down.'

He blushed and sat down. This mixture of eagerness and shyness in such a huge man was really something.

'Look here, Sardarji,' I said. 'This letter is from the Shraddhanand Orphaned Women's Institution. They say that at present there is no woman in their institution answering to the requirements in your letter. They will keep your application on file, and if they find a suitable

---

[2] Sir
[3] a respectful way to address a Sikh man

person for you, they will write and let you know. In the meantime, if it is possible, they would like you to come and see their manager.'

'H'mm,' he muttered, and then became silent.

'What is all this about, Sardarji?' I asked.

In a voice full of despair, he replied, 'It is not much to talk about, Janab.'

'But even then?'

'It is like this . . .' he began, but instantly changed his mind and said:

'I have already wasted a lot of your time, Huzur. Why should I waste more of it by narrating my worthless troubles?' There was a touch of pain on his face.

I did not like this shadow of sorrow on the face of one so full of health. My heart was filled with compassion and I placed a hand gently over his.

'There is no question at all of any waste of time, Sardarji. Quite the contrary. I shall consider it a privilege if I can be of some help to you in any way.'

He looked at me. He sensed my sympathy and smiled faintly.

'I am working here as a driver for the St. Peter's Girls' High School. White *Mem Sa'abs*[4] run that school and *Ingresi*[5] and *Parsi*[6] girls study there. The head Mem Sa'ab often asks me: 'Why do you not bring your wife here?'

'Are you married, then?' I asked in surprise.

'That is the whole trouble, *Sethji*,'[7] he said bitterly.

I became more and more intrigued. There was something extraordinary about the whole affair.

---

[4] European ladies
[5] English
[6] Indian community originally from Iran
[7] term of address for a Hindu businessman or a man of status

'I see,' I said untruthfully. 'Then, is it that they do not yet know you are not married?'

'If they knew it, do you think they would allow me to serve even for a minute in this girls' institution?' He laughed outright.

I also laughed. 'You are quite crafty and cunning, Sardar Sa'ab, not the simple straightforward one you outwardly appear.'

'What can one do, Janab? Life is so full of troubles.'

Some moments passed in silence. Then he continued with his tale.

'When I was discharged from the army. I had no job. The captain of my regiment, Jackson *Sa'ab*,[8] was well disposed towards me. I was not educated enough for a good job, but the Sahib knew that I was a good driver. This school was, at that time, in need of a driver. The Sahib knew it and recommended me to the Mem Sa'ab. She had no objection to taking me on provided I could satisfy her two requirements. First, my character should be irreproachable. Second, I should be married.

'Jackson Sa'ab came to me in a very jovial mood, after meeting the Mem, patted me lustily on the back, and roaring with laughter said: "Look here, Kartar Singh, I have made you a married man!"

'Had the Sahib gone mad? It seemed so for a moment, but I said politely: "Who would care to get the poor married, Captain Sa'ab?"

"I got you married just now," he repeated and roared with laughter again.

'I could not understand his mirth. Then he explained that he had secured the job for me by assuring the Mem that I satisfied both her requirements: my character was

[8] a European man, also a way of addressing an Indian man

irreproachable and – I was married. I was to start
working from the next day.

'A year has passed since then. The white lady often
asks me to bring my wife to see her. On one pretext or
another I postpone the evil day. But now it has become
difficult even to do that. If I want to continue in this job
any longer I must bring a wife here from wherever I
can. But I am a total stranger to these parts. Where am
I to bring a wife from?' He smiled wryly, and continued:

'Just by accident I met a kind gentleman the other
day. His name is Karsandasji. He talked about two or
three institutions in Bombay where it was possible to
get a wife. On my behalf he addressed some letters to
heads of those institutions; he left yesterday and I
received this letter today. And that, too, contains, as
you tell me, nothing but despair – only despair!' He
sighed.

'But Kartar Singh, why should you despair? You are
a stranger to these parts, but not to the Punjab. Why
don't you go there and get a wife?' I asked.

'Would I not have been married by now, if it was as
easy as that, Janab? I am already thirty-five.'

'Is it possible that you cannot get a girl from among
your own community and people?' I queried.

'Everything is possible where poor people are concerned, Huzur.'

I should not have laughed, for there was so much
sorrow and grief in his voice. Yet I could not restrain
myself.

'Then, according to you, all the poor people in the
world remain unmarried. Is that so, Sardarji?'

He also laughed with me. 'I may have exaggerated a
little, Sheth Sa'ab, but it is true in essence, particularly
in the case of a person like me. I left home early in
childhood and wandered here and there all over India.

Then I joined the army and fought in the war, and yet, what am I today? Almost a beggar, an insignificant driver in a girls' school in an out-of-the-way place. Now, who would care to give his daughter to a man like me?'

But the laughter vanished as he said with a tinge of grief in his voice:

'Thousands of poor people like me have to live and die without ever being able to marry, Huzur. How could happily-placed people like you know about these things?'

'If nobody feels inclined to give his daughter to you, let them go to hell,' I said, inclined to be facetious again. 'But a man like you, brave in war, strong and healthy, a man who has seen the big world outside, did not some girl out of her own free choice select you?'

'Oh, they? There are many like that, *Sarkar*.'[9] He straightened himself and a smile of victory floated reminiscently on his lips.

'Sure, sure, there must have been many. I swear! But then,' I joked on, 'why are you still the lonely bachelor you are?'

'*Kismet*,[10] *Kismet*, Huzur, it is all *Kismet*.'

'When our regiment was in Secunderabad we used to play football in a huge maidan. I do not know whether I looked very handsome then but it is a fact that one of the Christian girls residing in a house adjoining the football field got fond of me. I may appear vain as I say this,' he smiled, 'but it is the truth, Huzur. God's own truth. Well, she managed to get in touch with me and it was not long before she made her intentions known to me.'

[9] literally government; here used to mean 'governor' or 'boss'
[10] luck

'Was she beautiful?' I asked.

'Oh, she was beautiful as a goddess,' he assured me enthusiastically. But at that moment he perhaps saw the glint of a mischievous smile in my eyes and his extravagance subsided.

'Leave alone the goddess part of it, Huzur, but she was really very good-looking and very smart . . . hm . . . Seeing that she was trying to be intimate with me, I proposed to her.'

'Good, good, that was very good,' I applauded.

'She was prepared. She was just as poor as myself . . . we could have pulled together well.'

'Where, then, was the hitch?' I asked.

'She said she would marry me only if I became a Christian. She was not prepared to lose her religion on any account.'

'Really?' I asked, surprised.

'Yes, really. It is always like that, Janab. The converts always cling to their new faith very fanatically . . . She told me that if I became a Christian her parents and relatives would adopt me as their own and would very willingly agree to our marriage. But was that ever possible?'

'Why?'

'Why? Because if she was so proud of her own faith, I had also a faith which was in no way inferior to hers. Why should I change it? My ancestors had given their heads to defend that faith. I could not sacrifice it for this slip of a girl. I flatly said no. The matter ended there.'

'*Acchha*!'[11] I exclaimed.

'There was another adventure, too,' he said after some time.

[11] yes indeed

'Well.'

He shook his head. 'No, no, Janab, it is not worth telling. I myself was so disgusted with it . . . Well, once I was going to Poona from here by a local train. At Talegaon, a young Muslim woman, accompanied by a man, entered our compartment. The carriage was almost full, but somehow or the other they managed to seat themselves. Their seat was in a direction opposite to mine and at the other end.

'As the train moved on I felt that the woman was every now and then casting a glance in my direction. Though a Muslim, she was not in *purdah*.[12] I also looked at her. When our eyes met I could trace a faint pleasant smile on her lips. My hand automatically went to my moustache.'

'Ah, the hero!' I laughed. He felt embarrassed.

'I repented for it afterwards but I am, after all, a man . . . She cast her eyes down and smiled. So sweetly! That smile of hers lent beauty to her otherwise not beautiful face.'

'But what was the man with her doing all this time, while you two were playing out this little drama all for yourselves?'

'Looking out of the window and singing a song of passionate love,' Kartar Singh laughed.

'Before the train reached Poona she spread out her small handkerchief on her palm. I looked. Her name, Halima, was embroidered on it. I smiled at this trick of hers. She shyly turned away and crumpled the hanky in both her hands.

'When we got down at Poona she waved to me when nobody was looking at us. But my intoxication vanished at that moment. What was I doing? For mere pleasure,

[12] veil for screening women from being seen by men

was I spoiling the life of a married man? I – I who wanted to marry a decent faithful woman – I was doing that? Just for mere pleasure? I almost hated myself at that moment. That strong feeling took Halima completely out of my mind for ever.'

Kartar Singh ended his narrative, but that mixture of curiosity and fun with which I had till then been listening to him evaporated. A feeling of respect grew in my mind.

Reverting to the letter he had received, and from which all this talk had ensued, I said:

'Look here, Sardarji, you need not worry at all. I am going to Bombay tomorrow and will return here within a week. There, I shall make enquiries on your behalf. Had that Karsandasbhai written letters anywhere else besides?'

Kartar Singh's eyes shone with gratitude.

'I should not bother you more, Janab,' he said, but all the same, he drew out some letters from his pocket. Handing them over to me he said:

'Here, these are the letters.'

I read them. They were written to similar institutions for destitute women.

The demands of the Sardar were simple. He did not ask for beauty or youth, but only for a good, faithful Hindu or Sikh woman who would run his household peacefully and who had faith in God.

'I quite understand,' I said. 'In Bombay, I shall look for the kind of woman you want.'

We agreed to meet at the Lonavala market after eight days.

He thanked me profusely for the interest I had taken in him and went his way. I also hurriedly departed for my home as it was very late and people there might, perhaps, be worrying.

I went to Bombay the next day as arranged, and so much work was awaiting me there that for some days at least, I could not take myself off from it. To think of returning to Lonavala was out of the question. On the contrary, I had to recall my people from there to Bombay.

Poor Kartar Singh and his simple tale were entirely forgotten under the pressure of heavy work. When I got some respite, after some months, I did remember it – but soon I was lost in work again, and after so long it had lost for me the importance it had once seemed to possess. Thus time passed and I did nothing for him.

It was only after many months that I was able to return once more to my beloved Lonavala. Its fresh and invigorating air filled my lungs, and brought with it memories of days long past. Kartar Singh formed part of these memories and, as I remembered him, I felt both guilty and curious. Guilty because not only had I done nothing for him, I had not even had the courtesy, during all these months, to inform him that I could do nothing. Curious for obvious reasons. Had he found a woman be could marry? Or, had he lost his job because he could not find one? Was he still in Lonavala?

I could find answers to these questions by going to the market one evening, but my sense of guilt proved stronger. After my callous behaviour towards him I could not face the prospect of meeting him. So I avoided going near the market, particularly in the evenings.

Yet, despite my precautions, I could not avoid meeting him. One evening, as I was returning from my walk in the hills, I heard someone shouting to me from the direction of the Post Office. 'O Huzur! O Janab!'

I turned round. It was Kartar Singh. He was standing by a table in the restaurant where we had sat at our previous meeting, and he was shouting to me at the top of his voice – although his mouth was full of what he was eating. I hurried over to him and shook hands.

'How are you, Kartar Singh?'

'When did you return, Sheth Sa'ab? Do sit down, please. Have some tea.'

I took my seat and expressed regret that I had been unable to do anything for him.

'Oh, it is quite all right. Please don't worry about it.'

'You must be married by now, Sardarji?' I asked, after a pause.

Instantly, sorrow clouded his face. 'What marriage, Janab? Who would marry a penniless man like me? All want money.' Bitterly he repeated: 'Money.'

'What has happened, Sardar Sa'ab? Why do you appear so much disappointed?'

'It is nothing worth narrating. After you went away, I waited for a letter from you for about a month or so. Those were anxious days. After that I began to look out on my own. The Mem Sahib was insistent and – and –.' After some hesitation: 'Shall tell you the truth, Janab? I myself was thirsting for marriage. In the ordinary course, perhaps, I would not have thought of it, but having devoted so much thought to it during those days, I was actually feeling the need of a wife, children, home. Why should one not have them? How many precious years should one waste moving about alone on this earth? The softness of a woman's face, the sweetness of her voice, the grace of her movement, the joy of her love – all these things danced before my eyes every day. Even if the white Mem Sahib did not insist on my being a married man, even if my job did not depend upon it, I felt, intensely felt, that I should marry. But marriage was nowhere within sight. And, as you know, the greater the delay, the greater the desire.

'I went to Bombay myself. It was a job for me, a complete stranger in that huge city, to find out the institutions with which I had been corresponding. But, somehow or the other, I succeeded in tracking them down. I met the managers concerned. And at last,' he smiled bitterly, 'I arrived at one conclusion. A man in my position must have money if he ever hopes to marry. Honesty, truth, uprightness, character do not count.'

I remained silent, yet sympathetic. He continued: 'In some cases, Hindu women were not at all prepared to marry a Sikh. And in cases where they were so prepared the institution people would not allow them to – unless I deposited some money with them, or in a bank in the name of the women concerned. Where was I, a poor driver, to bring money from? And so I left it at that.'

'In no case . . .' I started to say something, but he intervened:

'Yes, in two or three cases there was no demand for money, but then those women were not worth marrying.'

'Kartar Singh,' I interrupted with a smile, 'did you not tell me that you did not care for beauty or age?'

'Yes, yes. Even now I say the same thing, but that does not mean that I did not require a good, pure, honest woman as my wife. These were women either rejected by their husbands for infidelity or were criminally inclined. How could I marry such women? Am I not happier as I am?'

'Then have you given up the idea of marriage altogether?' I asked.

'I do not know about that, but I am certain about one thing.'

'What is it?'

'That I shall have to leave this job after all.'

'Why?'

'How long can I carry on with one excuse or the

other? And how long can I go on inventing falsehoods? I have told the Mem my wife has gone to the Punjab to visit her family, but she cannot believe she would stay away from me for ever.'

That was true. I sat engrossed in thought for some moments. Then, all of a sudden, an idea flashed in my mind and I was filled with joy.

'Look here, Kartar Singh. I have an idea. You are right. How long can you go on sitting here and inventing excuses? That doesn't work. Well then, do as I tell you. You ask for leave for a month or two. Tell the Lady Superintendent that you want to go to the Punjab to fetch your wife.'

'Then?' he asked, curious.

'Then you try, really, to find a wife in those parts.'

'But if I fail?'

'It is easy enough even then.' I said enthusiastically. 'When you get back, you can say that some days before your return your wife fell ill, and the relatives would not hear of sending her away in that condition. That way you will get a lease of some more months. Can't a real marriage be arranged during that time?'

'Yes, that sounds well enough,' he said thoughtfully. Then, gradually, he too was filled with enthusiasm.

'Yes, yes, that is quite true. Within a year at the most, even if I have to go to the end of the earth, I shall certainly find a wife for myself.' Then he added with a smile: 'I do not like to be without her even a moment. Will she dare delay for a whole year?' The smile remained as he pondered. 'The Punjab is full of young girls, and I can earn bread for two.'

The idea took root and within four or five days after that Kartar Singh left for the Punjab. I went to the station to see him off. He was full of hope and his optimism was infectious.

'Kartar Singh, I wish you all success in your mission,' I said sincerely.

All of a sudden he was full of the old anxiety.

'If I fail this time also, I shall feel very miserable. I hate living alone now,' he murmured.

'Why speak of failure? You will succeed, I am sure,' I said, and the train started on its journey.

During the following months I often remembered his face, eager, hopeful, anxious. I often felt curious about what had happened to him. Accordingly when some time later I again went to Lonavala, almost the first thought that came to me was to visit him as soon as I could. That very evening I found him in the market-place.

I saw immediately that he was looking unhappy and I suggested he come with me to the restaurant if he were in no particular hurry.

On the way he said sorrowfully:

'Nothing came of it, brother.'

I did not know what to say. His sorrow imparted itself to me. We reached the restaurant in silence. It was not until we sat at a table that he began:

'I tried my utmost, but why bother about that? When I returned here alone I told the Mem Sa'ab what you had taught me. On hearing that my wife was ill the Mem Sa'ab was all sympathy. She offered me some money so that I could treat my wife. I, of course, declined. How could I add that sin to the many false-hoods I had uttered? I merely said that my wife would certainly follow within about two months' time.

'While talking to her, Janab, I had a certain inspira-tion.' Kartar Singh's face beamed with joy in the midst of his tale of sorrow as he added: 'After some three months I went to her and told her with shyness in my voice that I had received a letter from my people. It said that my wife was with child and my people would not send her here now. What then should I do? The Mem was mightily pleased.'

'Really? That was very clever of you,' I said.

'The Mem Sahib is such a great lady. It is only since I met her that I have come to realise that there are people on this earth directly related to God. "All right, Kartar Singh," she said, "it is quite all right. Let the child be born there. Then you bring him here. We shall teach him some very good things here."

'She is overjoyed at the thought of my becoming a father. Daily she instructs me to write to my wife about things she should and should not do at this delicate time of her life. So, Janab, for the present there is nothing to worry about so far as my job is concerned.'

'But what will you say after some time has passed? Have you thought about that?' I asked.

He was miserable again. 'What can I think, Janab?' After a painful moment he added: 'Shall I tell you the truth, Huzur? My hopes, yes, even my desire to marry, are now dead, really dead.'

I do not know whether that word 'dead' gave me the idea but I said:

'Do one thing then, Kartar Singh. Tell the Mem Sahib that your wife died in childbirth.'

For a time Kartar Singh sat there dumb, with downcast eyes, very much engrossed in thought. He did not even appear to have heard what I had said. So much grief and sorrow had clouded his face that I did not like to disturb him.

Then, his lips opened and closed silently. It seemed as though he were taking a decision about something.

At last, he raised his face. My eyes met his. And his were full of the gloom that one experiences at the passing away of a very near and dear one.

Being unable to gaze for a long time at the grief in his face, I looked away. As soon as I turned my eyes from him, he said in a voice full of pathos:

'You speak the truth, Janab. Now she is really dead.'

The desolation in his voice pained me almost unbearably. As I looked at him again, he rose from the table.

'She is really dead now,' he repeated slowly, and walked away.

A vast emptiness swelled inside me and I could not move for a minute. When I followed him outside he had disappeared. But his footsteps left the echoes of many such deaths!

Sunita Jain

A Dead Wife

Mr Varma, the attorney living next door, is getting married today. I'm depressed, I feel like picking a quarrel with him. Maybe it will make me feel better. The thing is, I am still unmarried and very sensitive about it.

Mr Varma's bungalow is situated such, that, sitting on our porch, I can see most of what goes on in there. The fence between the two houses broke down a few years ago and was never repaired. Both our families were so friendly that neither wanted to bother – and it was easier to visit each other.

I can see that everything is ready, the procession is about to start. Two men are sprinkling water from leather buckets onto the red gravel, to keep the dust low. It's quite a large gathering of relatives and friends. But I have decided not to attend his wedding – even if Mother gets upset. How shameful for him to marry within two months of Mrs Varma's death!

As I had expected, Mother was not happy to see me sitting on the porch. 'Good Lord! Don't you want to be there on time? The procession is going to start and you're still sitting there holding a book! I don't understand you any more!'

'Mother, I'm not going. But you go ahead; don't wait for me.'

'But why? They're our neighbours, and they'll certainly be hurt. What shall I tell them?'

'Anything, Mother. I'm not going.'

'At least – tell me why? I haven't even prepared dinner; you'll have to go hungry.'

'I'm not hungry. Mother, I'm surprised at you, too. You loved Mrs Varma – and as soon as she dies you dress up for Mr Varma's wedding!' I couldn't go on. Mother sat down next to me.

'No one can change fate, darling. I loved Kamla more than I love my own sisters!' Her voice had a melancholy tone.

'What really shocked me, Mother, was that Mr Varma would get married so soon . . . .'

'Don't blame him, dear. I'm sure he isn't too happy, either. Didn't you see how he cared for Kamla when she was sick! He is getting married for the sake of the children.'

'The children! It's all a pretence, Mother. A stepmother won't make them happy. He's so rich; why doesn't he hire someone for them – a governess, I mean?'

'A governess will never be the same as a mother. You're too young to understand. Why do you think she won't love them? Just because she's a stepmother? People aren't all like that. You're angry, that's all. Varma has his work; he can't take care of babies! With a wife he won't have to worry about his children.'

'Suppose she doesn't love his children.'

'Then that's their fate. Otherwise their own mother wouldn't have died. Darling, when I got married your grandmother gave me your eldest brother as a wedding gift! He was only eighteen months. Ask him if he missed his mother for a moment. I still love him more than I love all of you combined!'

What Mother said was a fact. Anyway, when I argue with her I always lose! She's gone to the wedding and the procession has started. I am still sitting here and listening to the loud pop music for the wedding. I have heard that recorded music in marriage ceremonies is already outdated in big cities like New Delhi; but Meerut is not that advanced. I wonder why the authorities don't levy a tax on those who disturb other people's peace and sleep. I have a headache.

The bride arrived this afternoon. A new-born baby and a bride are my greatest weaknesses; I can't help peeking at them. I forgot my anger for a while and went over to see her. Usually, a bride is surrounded by all the women of the house. But Mrs Varma was sitting in a corner, almost alone. She wore a red cotton saree and looked uncomfortable. Her veil came up to the tip of her nose. I lifted the veil and stared. She was hardly seventeen or eighteen! Her eyes were swollen and red from constant crying, and she kept staring at her toes. She had a very fresh and healthy complexion.

I noticed that the family wasn't very curious about her. Firstly, because she was a 'second,' and then she came from a poor family. Her dowry consisted mostly of cotton sarees. Everyone was busy eating and joking. Those who were curious were Mr Varma's six children; they came by turns, and looked with awe at their new mother. That awe told me that they'd been fully prepared for a stepmother.

I returned home bursting with anger, and immediately poured it out on Mother!

'You see, Mother! You were so sympathetic to poor Mr Varma! What right did he have to marry such a girl?'

'What happened?'

'He's halfway to the grave and married to a girl younger than myself!'

'Shame, Geeta! Don't talk like that! He's only forty!'

'Double – more than double – her age! Mother! It's unjust! She's only a child and she'll have to care for six children. She looks like their elder sister, not their mother! I'm so upset, Mother, that I can hardly bear it. Tell me – ish't it awful to marry a widower?'

I bit my tongue. But it was too late. Mother didn't say anything. As I stood there, ashamed and uncertain, she quietly wiped her eyes to keep tears from falling into the dough she was kneading.

There's a transmitter between our house and Mr Varma's which brings the up-to-the-minute news with running commentary. It's a live transmitter – our servant, Jugni, the woman who does the cleaning for both houses. The first comments that we heard were: 'The new bride really belongs to the lower class. She has no shame or dignity. She lifted her veil the very next day, and is roaming all over the house like a man. She's also sending all Mr Varma's aunts, who'd been in the house for months, back to where they belong.'

I was surprised, and my surprise kept her talking.

'Don't be astonished, Geeta. She just doesn't know what she's supposed to do as the lady of the house. I think she comes from a village, where she worked, ate, and slept. I'm sure that within a week she'll send the cook packing, too. God help the children! Gone are the days of the first Mrs Varma!'

I was worried, too, especially for the baby Pintoo, whom I love dearly. I was wondering if the new Mrs Varma would be unkind to such a small baby. I felt frustrated that I could not do anything. What right did I have anyway?

In the afternoon, we heard that Mr Varma had gone to court looking very pale. And all the guests were leaving, and 'the bride' was getting the house thoroughly cleaned! I caught hold of the eldest boy and asked, 'Binnoo, how's your mother? Do you like her?'

'I don't know!' He ran away.

I usually get up very late in the morning. When I got up the next day I peeked into the house next to ours. It was all very quiet. The children were nowhere in sight. On other days I could see them playing and quarrelling all day long.

I finished breakfast and came out; I was in for a surprise. All the five boys seemed very clean and tidy, and they were sitting in a row. Mr Shastri, our school teacher, was looking at them! As I looked on, perplexed, Jugni came out and whispered, 'See what I told you! The cook was gone this morning, and now the teacher has come, so the children can't even enjoy the rest of their vacation!'

At about two in the afternoon Binnoo came to borrow mother's sewing machine. Mother was surprised.

'Sewing machine! What will you do with it, Binnoo?'

'Auntie . . . Mother wants it. She wants to sew some under-clothes for Pintoo and Mikky.'

'In this weather? It's boiling hot outside. This is no time to make clothes. What was she doing in the morning, when it was cool?'

'She was cooking, Auntie. The cook's gone.'

'Oh, I had forgotten!'

Mother seemed very worried. She was talking to herself.

'Something's surely wrong. Haven't heard or seen a bride like that . . . .'

About two days later Pintoo was sitting in my lap; I was reading a magazine that had arrived that morning. Mother asked, 'Pintoo, what's your mother doing?'

'Oh, Aunt, I forgot to tell you. Mother has built a beautiful temple in her room. And she has Lord

Krishna's statue, about this high. She prays in the morning and sleeps there at night, and I sleep with her. Mother says if I sleep in the temple I won't have bad dreams . . . .'

My mother sat stunned for a few minutes, then suddenly got up and went across the lawn.

I went on reading; Pintoo fell asleep in my lap. She was getting so heavy that I decided to take her home and put her to bed. As I put her down, she caught my saree and wouldn't let go. This was her old trick. I stayed with her, patting her slowly, until she was fast asleep. The window was open, and I could hear Mother and Mrs Varma in the next room. Mother was saying, 'You should take care of yourself, dear. You'll make yourself sick this way.'

'Auntie, I'm all right. Please don't worry about me!' Mother becomes a 'relation' so quickly! Her generosity and love seem inexhaustible.

'No, I don't think that you're all right! Why did you dismiss the cook? Now you have to do the cooking yourself.'

'Somehow, Auntie, it didn't seem right for me to do nothing and the family to eat food cooked by a servant. And I wanted to hire a tutor for the children!'

'The schools haven't opened yet.'

'I know. But when I cleaned the house all their books were torn and in bad shape. So I decided to get them ready . . . .'

'And when did you plan this temple? And I don't think you look like a bride. There's hardly any jewellery on you. Even this saree is terrible!'

'I don't mind it – Auntie!' But Mother didn't hear. She went on, 'And I've heard that you sleep here too!' It seemed Mother couldn't wait any longer.

There was no answer.

'Where does Mr Varma sleep?'

'In his room.'

'In the study?'

'Yes!'

'Now what's that! You sleeping with the children and he in his room! How long have you been married? Four days! Listen to me, darling; tell me if something is the matter . . . I'm old enough to be your mother. You're so young . . . Tell me if I can help? . . .'

I heard muffled sobs. Mother was trying to soothe the bride. I couldn't make out anything for a while, it was all drowned in crying. Then I heard Mrs Varma saying, '. . . Night of our wedding, he said, "Take care of my children. They are yours too, now. God has already given me six. I've made arrangements . . . I had myself operated on a few days ago . . . so that we won't have more . . ."'

'What! Operated!'

'Yes, Auntie. But I'm very grateful to him. He told me. Otherwise, I would have died! Now I'm happy. I've given myself to Lord Krishna!'

'What are you talking about?'

'Auntie, I'm a very simple, uneducated girl. All that I've studied are some religious books and they say that relations between a man and a woman are for the reproduction of life, which is our sacred duty. Otherwise, it's vice, it's lust . . . I told him I'd take good care of his children, and he'd have no complaint, but he could never touch me . . .'

I heard a sob which was more like a heart breaking. She was saying, in a voice which cut my heart, 'To that sister of mine, his wife, he gave six, Auntie, but he cannot give me one! Only one, just so that my life wouldn't be wasted . . .'

I didn't have the courage to hear any more. I sat there plastered to the floor, my knees too weak to carry me.

To the Teacher

Pupils must be provided with opportunities to read literary, non-literary and media texts, some of which should be whole works, and to show an informed engagement with the work of a wide range of authors from a variety of cultures and times.[1]

This book has been compiled both to extend the scope of literature in the English curriculum and also with the belief that enjoyment will be part of the reward of studying the stories included. Several equally important criteria have formed the basis on which the stories have been selected: their literary merit; their accessibility to readers regardless of their cultural background; their capacity to promote valuable cultural understanding of South Asian people;[2] their variety of styles, approaches and viewpoints which make them appropriate for the study of the short story as a genre; their suitability to meet the oral and written course work requirements of examination courses in secondary schools as well as sixth form colleges; their relevance as part of the wider reading of students preparing for the GCSE, GCSE (17) as well as A Level examination courses; their capacity to transcend cultural boundaries despite their

---

[1] 'GCSE Criteria for English – Applicable to examinations in and from 1994', (School Examinations and Assessment Council, 1990) – para. 3.6
[2] 'South Asia' here refers to India, Pakistan and Bangladesh.

origins in South Asia, and therefore their pertinence and value to us here now.

Although each story can be looked at independently, they have been grouped, as suggested in the Contents list, to facilitate comparative study. 'A Devoted Son' and 'Smoke', for instance, while exploring how the filial sense of duty carried too far can have ironic consequences for the persons involved, also reveal interesting aspects of two Hindu families and the role definition of the central characters. 'The Bhorwani Marriage', with its satirical narrator, gives us critical insight into the procedures leading to the arranged marriage of a young couple, while 'The Bride', which is a witty feminist fable, not only forms a striking contrast stylistically with the preceding story but invites the reader to reconsider the distribution of power in the relationships between male and female members of families as well as in society as portrayed in both stories. The human desire and need for companionship and the degree to which the mores of society can frustrate individual fulfilment form the central concerns of the next story in the collection, 'Too Late for Anger', which also features the conflict between traditional and modern values and lifestyles – a theme it shares with 'The First Party'. As with many other stories here, irony lends depth and significance to the meanings the reader can construct from the text. I hope these examples illustrate the approach adopted in this anthology.

Because the stories can accommodate different readings and/or emphases, it is quite feasible to group the stories differently, and this in itself is an interesting area for exploration through discussion and essay writing: the classroom activities cover this flexibility in the arrangement of the stories. Two other aspects are also worth mentioning here: firstly, nine of these stories were originally written in English; one was reconceived by the author (Gulabhdas Broker) from the Gujarati into English; another one was recreated from Bengali into English by the author (Rabindranath Tagore) in collaboration with another writer; and five stories (as indicated on the first page where relevant) are in translation. Once again this provides another area of useful investigation: on the one hand, the varieties of English in use among them serve to remind the reader of the richness and eclectic nature of English as a world language, and on the other hand, particular stories employ a recognisably Indian use of English while revealing an unmistakeably Indian sensibility. Essay titles I have listed pick up this area. Secondly, the extent to which a story in translation can successfully convey the thoughts, feelings, attitudes and social situations of people from another culture forms the basis of another essay title. (Readers familiar with the June 1989 Report of the Cox Committee – 'English for ages 5 to 16' – will know its recommendation that 'works in translation may also be included' in the literary range offered to students: paragraph 7.18.)

Part of the editorial thinking in compiling this collection was to ensure a balance in the representation of male and female authors: eight stories by each are included. As the final selection took shape, an interesting pattern began to emerge: well-known and highly acclaimed authors of the past generation (such as Abbas, Broker, Manto, Narayan and Tagore) find themselves placed alongside distinguished contemporary authors (such as Das, Desai, Mehta, Namjoshi and Perera): the majority in the first group comprise male writers, whilst female writers dominate the second group. This not only makes it possible for male and female perspectives to be juxtaposed through stories on

147

related themes but allows comparison of past and present points of view, yet without the sense of any of the stories being dated.

The stories lend themselves to study at different levels which make them suitable for mixed ability groups. They range from the straightforward to the deceptively simple but demanding. All repay careful consideration and the classroom activities are designed to enhance the reading process, to help students become critically aware of literary aspects such as narrative technique, point of view and the writer's intentions, style and structure, to open up the possibility of different readings and/or emphases, to examine the short story as a genre, to encourage and support oral as well as written work on the many social, cultural, moral and political issues raised by the stories, to speculate on the extent to which particular stories are culture-specific and the respects in which many express universals, and finally, to go beyond the compass of the single story to wider concerns where possible. The stories, then, are introduced here at two levels: as literature and as a contribution to multicultural education:

> An active involvement with literature enables pupils to share the experience of others. They will encounter and come to understand a wide range of feelings and relationships by entering vicariously the worlds of others, and in consequence they are likely to understand more of themselves.[3]

Where appropriate, glossaries have been included with the stories. The *before, during* and *after* reading format of

[3] The Cox Report: 'English for Ages 5 to 16: Proposals of the Secretary of State for Education and Science and the Secretary of State for Wales' (DES), June 1989 – para. 7.3

the follow-on activities means that teachers may find it very helpful to preview the suggested approaches before they introduce a story. It should be noted that these suggestions are offered in the hope that they are helpful: they are not prescriptive and teachers and students are invited to adopt or adapt them to their own purposes. I have assumed that students may wish to work collaboratively, but of course they may also do so independently.

Madhu Bhinda

Activities

A Devoted Son

Before you start reading

1 If you were old and ill, would you want to be kept alive by modern medicine? Discuss in groups.

2 Should the very ill and elderly be allowed to die or should hospitals and doctors do their best to keep them alive? Hold a class discussion.

During reading

3 Pause after reading 'for a night under the stars.' (page 10). On your own or with a partner, make a brief note of those actions that show that the son is devoted to his father. This will help you to judge, later, how far the title relates to the story.

After reading

4 Which of the following statements about the story do you agree with? Discuss them with your partner(s) and place them in two columns – those you agree with, and those you disagree with. When you finish, exchange your views with other groups.

(a) Rakesh was a perfect son to his parents.

(b) Rakesh wanted to keep his father alive as long as possible.

(c) The father did not appreciate his son's efforts.

(d) The father would have lived on happily if he was allowed to have the food he was fond of.

(e) The father wanted to die because he felt unloved.

(f) The father was too ill and too frail to want to stay alive.

(g) Rakesh showed perfect duty as a son and a doctor, but no love for his father.

(h) The title does not fit the story!

(i) The old and ill deserve to have their wishes respected even if what they want is not good for them.

(j) Duty without love can be unkind.

Add other statements of your own if you wish to.

5 Imagine old Varma asks you to put his case – to be allowed to die – to his son Rakesh. Rakesh will naturally put his own arguments to you (as a son and as a doctor). Write out your conversation with Rakesh in play-form or as a story.

6 Write an essay in which you discuss the relationship between the title and the story.

7 Do you think euthanasia should be legalised? Talk about the issue and then write an essay giving your views on the topic.

See also Activities 1 and 2 in the section 'Compare and Contrast Stories' on page 187.

Smoke

Before you start reading

1 In groups talk about your experiences of that short time *before* specially invited visitors arrive for dinner. Everything is ready, so there is nothing to do but wait. How do people you know behave as they wait?

> *Note:*
> *It is suggested you look at the story in three sections:*
> *Section 1: From the start to page 18, stopping after 'a dark blot to you.'*
> *Section 2: Page 19, from 'Suddenly her belly tightened. . . .' to page 20, stopping at 'in a road accident.'*
> *Section 3: The rest of the story.*

During reading

2 Read the first section of the story. Then discuss with your partner(s) how you think Shubha is feeling. How can you tell?

3 Read the second section of the story. What can we tell about the relationships in this Hindu family from this passage? Discuss the following relationships with your partner(s):
   – Shubha and Ba
   – Shubha and Subodh
   – Ba and her son and husband (Subodh and Bapuji)

4 Now, with your partner(s), try to decide which of the following statements might explain Ba's probable disapproval of Shubha's smoking.
   (a) Ba didn't know about it.
   (b) Shubha is a doctor and should know better!
   (c) Smoking is offensive to Ba's traditional Hindu beliefs.
   (d) Subodh and Bapuji might have disapproved of it.
   Add any other reasons you can think of.

After reading

5 The following suggested reasons may explain why Shubha smokes. If you agree with them, put them in order of priority with your partner(s), placing the strongest reason at the top and the weakest at the bottom of your list:

(a) She is lonely.
(b) Her life feels 'empty' because she has recently become a widow.
(c) She is tense because Ba may discover her secret habit (if Ba finds out, both women will be upset for different reasons).
(d) Shubha finds her work as a doctor depressing.
(e) Shubha is attracted to another man but feels unable to develop this relationship.
(f) She is admired as a saint-like person and feels trapped in this role.

6 Decide with your partner(s) which of these two statements best sums up this story:
(a) It is about a woman who wishes to begin a new life, but is trapped by her past.
(b) It shows the conflict between old and new attitudes about how to cope with life.
Add other statements if you wish to.

7 Continue writing the story from where it leaves off.

8 Imagine Shubha keeps a diary. Write down her thoughts and feelings that night as she goes to bed. You may like to refer to the following:
– the discovery of her habit as a smoker
– her relationship with/responsibility to her mother-in-law
– her life as a widow and a doctor
– her friendship with Latika's brother
– her hopes for the future.

See also Activities 1, 2 and 3 in the section 'Compare and Contrast Stories' on page 187.

The Bhorwani Marriage

Before you start reading
1 Hold a class discussion on horoscopes and your

beliefs/scepticism about them, perhaps along these lines:

(a) How many of you read horoscopes regularly or frequently?

(b) How many of you take them seriously?

(c) Would you base important decisions in your life on horoscope forecasts – such as a choice of career or marriage partner?

During reading

2 Read the first two pages of the story (pages 28–29) carefully. Now decide with your partner(s) what the narrator's attitude to his clients is. Is he:

(a) poking gentle fun at them?

(b) seriously critical of them?

(c) making fun of them in order to criticise them, ie. being satirical?

(d) business-like and shrewd?

3 Decide also which of these descriptions apply to the narrator. Is he:

(a) honest with the reader?

(b) honest with his clients?

(c) clever – knows how to get what he wants?

(d) critical?

(e) humorous?

(f) serious?

After reading

4 How far do you agree with the following statements about the story? Discuss them with your partner(s):

(a) It is about a few days in the busy life of a marriage broker called a 'maharaj'.

(b) It shows how marriages are arranged for the children of a very rich minority.

(c) It shows the bargaining done by the interested parties.

(d) A marriage can take place *only* if a boy agrees with the choice of a girl for him.

(e) A girl can disagree with the choice of a boy for her.

(f) A girl has to bring a dowry as her contribution to the family she joins upon marriage.

(g) The amount of the dowry is settled by bargaining: the wealthier the family, the bigger the dowry.

(h) Doing away with the dowry system may give girls an equal status to the boys.

(i) The Maharaj tries to arrange weddings for the children of the rich whenever possible because he will get a big arranger's fee.

(j) Marriages are arranged because boys and girls are not expected to meet freely as they do in European countries.

(k) Matching horoscopes for the boy and girl suggests that they may share a happy future.

(l) Mothers exercise considerable power in their families and in arranged marriages, even though women are to be considered less than equal to men in society.

5 Reread the two paragraphs starting on page 35 with 'The inevitable Apollo . . .' and finishing after 'they held similar views on life.' Now imagine you are the girl or the boy and that this is your first opportunity to get to know the person you may marry. Write out the conversation that takes place on the seafront. You may write it in the form of a story if you wish.

6 Read the article on page 156 – 'Wanted: farm hands for life'. Then write an essay discussing the following:

(a) How far does a marriage bureau perform the same functions as the marriage broker we met in 'The Bhorwani Marriage'?

(b) Bearing in mind the special difficulties of farmers

Wanted: farm hands for life

by Mazhar Mahmood and Hugh Clayton

COUNTRY life is a lonely life, according to hundreds of farmers who are flocking to new agricultural marriage bureaux, desperately seeking wives.

Specialist journals like Horse & Hound and the Farmers Weekly have begun printing columns of lonely heart ads appealing for country-loving partners, and a number of existing farmers' wives are turning rural shyness into a lucrative business by setting up dating agencies.

William Lowe, 45, has been keenly searching for a partner since his 20-year marriage broke up a year ago. He owns a 400-acre farm in the West Midlands which has an annual turnover of more than £100,000.

At his luxurious farmhouse, complete with swimming pool and disco, he said: 'I tried to go out and meet potential partners but I didn't know where to begin. At my age and living in a secluded environment it's virtually impossible to meet the right person.'

Lowe, who met his first wife at a country dance, placed a discreet advertisement in the journal of the Country Landowners' Association. He also joined two dating agencies for lonely farmers.

'It was a bit embarrassing at first but many of my friends in similar circumstances have now joined agencies,' he said. 'It's a bit like buying a second-hand tractor. You have to put yourself about to get the right machine.'

One of the agencies contacted by Lowe is run by Heather Heber-Percy, who in eight months has interviewed more than 600 men aged between 25 and 80. They have nearly as many divorced and separated women on their books, many of them running their own smallholdings.

Heber-Percy, who runs the business from her home in Ludlow, Shropshire, said: 'Finding compatible partners for people living or working in the country is a major dilemma, particularly for the divorced.

'With the advent of television and video, farm dances and country fêtes have disappeared and there is no opportunity for couples to meet. Besides, farm workers work such unsociable hours.'

Heber-Percy admitted that the kind of lifestyle many men on her books had in mind would horrify women. A farmer's wife can expect to have to get up before dawn, drive the children several miles to school, and help in daily farm tasks ranging from milking cows and shearing sheep to cleaning stables. She may handle all the administration and paperwork on the farm, and will probably seldom go on holiday.

But there are no immediate plans for a marriage bureau in Britain's best-known country community, Ambridge. A spokesman for The Archers, the BBC radio series, said: 'Although Jo Grundy has advertised for a wife, there is no shortage of women. However, we cannot rule out the possibility of introducing a marriage bureau in the future.'

The Sunday Times: 27 December 1987

(and perhaps other working people in similar circumstances, eg shift workers), discuss the merits of each of the following ways to help these people:
- a marriage bureau;
- a marriage broker;
- arranged marriages.

Can you think of any other ways?

Which of the above do you consider to be the best method?

See also Activity 5 in the section 'Compare and Contrast Stories' on page 187.

The Bride

Before you start reading

1 How do fairy stories typically begin and end? Hold a class discussion.

2 As a class, brainstorm quick responses to this question: what ideas do you think of when someone speaks about 'womanly qualities'?

(Alternatively, brainstorm responses to the same question in single sex small groups in the class. Then collate your responses on the blackboard for comparison.)

During reading

3 As you read the story, consider whether you think this is a typical fairy story.

After reading

4 How is 'The Bride' different from a typical fairy story? Discuss.

Discuss Activities 5–9 with your partner(s) and make brief notes:

5 You may have noticed that the author has chosen to leave out the setting of the story as well as the

names of the characters. How do you think this is significant?

6 At least two kinds of women are mentioned in this story. Can you identify these?

7 What do you think the prince means when he says he prefers women with 'womanly qualities'? Why does he reject the other women? How similar/ different are your ideas about 'womanly qualities' compared to his?

8 What are the differences between the power of the men as against the women in this fable?

9 A fable is a story with a moral or a 'message'. Suggest what moral(s) or 'message(s)' you think the author intended in this fable.

Would the moral(s) have been the same if the author were male?

10 Bearing in mind the unequal distribution of power in this fable, rewrite it so that the balance of power is no longer concentrated on men. (You will need to decide which details to change and how else the story will develop differently.)

11 When you finish, comment on your own reconstructed story.
    – Explain two or three important ways in which you have changed the original story (use quotations and comment on them to show your thinking).
    – Is power now fairly distributed in the relationships between women and men?
    – What moral(s) come through to the reader from your version of the story?

12 Your reading of 'The Bride' may well alter the way you now see 'The Bhorwani Marriage'. With your partner, compare and contrast the two stories, and where appropriate, explore how your reading of the one affects your reading of the other.

You may find the following helpful in developing your discussion:
- the story openings;
- the narrative technique;
- the attitude of each author to the characters;
- settings and character names;
- what the stories have in common;
- how they are different;
- the distribution of power in the relationships between women and men;
- the use of humour;
- the story endings;
- your views of the authors' intentions in writing these stories.

See also Activity 6 in the section 'Compare and Contrast Stories' on page 187.

Too Late for Anger

Before you start reading
1 Discuss with your partner(s) which of these two statements is more true for you:
   (a) Your life becomes what you make of it.
   (b) Your life becomes what society lets you make of it.
2 Brainstorm ideas to interpret the title of this story. What can you predict about the story from it? What sort of mood does the title suggest to you?

During reading
3 Pause after reading the first three paragraphs. Stories are not always told in natural time order: consider with your partner(s) how the author/narrator moves back and forth in time in the first three paragraphs of the story.

4 As you read, consider too what period of time the story covers. This will help you to judge how slowly or rapidly developments occur in this story.

After reading

5 Very early in the story, the author alerts us to the sad decline in the lives of the Kirits. Reread paragraphs three and four. Then, with your partner, make notes about the eventual state of affairs, choosing two quotations which suggest this.

6 Decide which of these statements about the Kirit family your group agrees with.

The Kirits were a close family because:

(a) they loved each other;
(b) the sudden death of their parents made them look to each other for emotional support;
(c) they lacked the courage to go separate ways;
(d) if Meena and Lena had been able to get married, Raj too would have found himself a wife;
(e) society's narrow-minded gossiping meant that they could not live as they would have wished to;
(f) single people have a harder time than married ones.

Add other reasons you can think of to the list above.

7 After the rejection of Meena, Raj says:

> *Our girls are given the education and ideals to believe in freedom, but never the circumstances and encouragement to carry it out, to live what they believe. It's a sham all round . . .*

Raj blames society. Do you think he is right, or do you think Meena was to blame?

8 The story suggests that if Meena and Lena had been less well educated, they would have found husbands

more easily, meaning that men prefer their wives not to be their equals, or worse, better qualified. Do you think this is true in our society? If so, why do think this is the case?

9 The author points out the irony of how the sisters had been tutored not to be 'different', and actually 'of how different they had eventually become from most of their contemporaries.' (page 51)

How does the fate of the Kirit family make you feel? Sad? Angry? Frustrated? Sympathetic? All of these?

Explain your feelings and try to decide how suitable you think the author's title is for the story.

10 Write an essay in which you discuss the relationship between the title and story.

11 Reread the following four paragraphs from 'Soon he did know. . . .' (page 48) to, 'her degree will keep her warm at night.'

Imagine Gopal, the Brahmin professor, writes a letter of explanation to Lena after their relationship is ended. Construct his letter, as well as Lena's reply.

(Remember that the tone of each letter will probably be quite different. Decide about this before you begin.)

See also Activities 8, 11 and 12 in the section 'Compare and Contrast Stories' on page 187.

The First Party

Before you start reading
1 In small groups, talk about how you felt and coped when you went to your first party as a teenager. Try

to recall the kinds of things you felt nervous or anxious about.

2 Because of the author's very economical style of writing, you will be requested to reread parts of the story for a careful consideration of their content.

During reading

3 Read up to: 'and she smiled to hide them' (page 54) and pause to make very brief notes on the following with your partner(s):
   (a) At what point does the story begin?
   (b) Is the narrator in the story or outside it?
   (c) From whose viewpoint does the story appear to be written?
   (d) How does the narrator feel toward the woman? How can you tell?
   (e) Do we know for how long the visiting couple have been married?
   (f) For what reasons does the Indian woman feel nervous? (You will find several reasons!)

After reading

4 You may have noticed that the author does not name any of the characters. How is this significant? Discuss with your partner(s) and make notes.

5 Reread the passage beginning 'She did not know whether . . .' (page 54) and stop after 'when anyone came near.' (page 55) With your partner(s), note down the different reasons why the woman feels uncomfortable and culturally isolated (even from her husband).

6 What would you say is the husband's attitude to his wife from the above passage? Discuss with your partner and make notes.

7 How fair would it be to say that the woman's distress is created by her husband? Discuss with your partner and make notes.

8 Reread the passage on page 57 beginning 'A few couples began to dance . . .' and ending on page 58 with 'a safe path through unknown dangers.'

Does your sympathy lie with the woman or her husband? Explain your views.

The last short paragraph from the passage you have just read is worth noting for its careful wording. Pick out what you consider to be the key words and then decide which of these statements you would agree with:

(a) The author suggests that the woman sees no future with her newly acquired husband.

(b) The author sympathises with the woman but criticises her strict upbringing.

(c) The rules of behaviour by which she was brought up seemed restrictive at the time; now she recognises them to be sensible – they were a guard against moral danger.

(d) The husband should have taken into account his wife's background: his lack of consideration has caused his wife great unhappiness and put their relationship at risk.

9 Imagine you are the Indian woman at this party. Write out your thoughts and feelings, starting at the point where 'A few couples began to dance . . .' on page 57, and continuing through till the end of the story; (You will need to convert as much as possible of the author's writing into your own inner language.)

10 Continue writing the story from where it stops. Your main characters will be the husband and his wife.

11 Reconstruct the story, or a portion of it, from the husband's point of view.

12 Attia Hosain demonstrates how a story written in Standard English can convincingly show aspects of another culture. How far do you agree or disagree with this statement? Write an essay giving your reasons.

13 Suppose the husband and wife switch roles in this story, so that she has the good time at the party and he sits and watches, too shy to participate. Rewrite the story, or a portion of it, from his point of view.

14 Suppose the Indian woman chose to speak to you as a friend about her first party experience. Write out your conversation. You will need to decide what role you will play: sympathetic adviser, kindly listener, an unsympathetic critic – or something else?

For a further essay title, see Activity 12 in the section 'Compare and Contrast Stories' (page 187).

Overcoat

Before you start reading

1 In groups, discuss these questions and make brief notes on them:

  (a) We all tend to judge people by their appearance: how true is this for you and other people you know?

  (b) How much can you tell about a person from their appearance?

  (c) Could people be rejected because of what they look like?

You may wish to come together in your groups to share views.

2 Now brainstorm ideas to predict what you can about the story from the title.

ACTIVITIES

During reading

3 Read the first three paragraphs of this story with care. Discuss with your partner(s) and briefly note down your impressions of the man from the details in these paragraphs.

4 Although this story is a work of fiction, you will notice that the author uses precise place names as the young man proceeds about his walk. Try to decide with your partner why you think the author chose to do this – what does it do for the story?

After reading

5 Briefly discuss responses to Activity 4 above.

Work on questions 6–9 with your partner(s) and make brief notes:

6 What conclusions do you draw from the way people treat the young man as they meet him (for example, in the music shop or the carpet shop).

7 You will have noticed that the author concentrates on an external description of the young man. We have little access to his inner thoughts and feelings. How is this significant?

8 The author does not name the young man. Is this because:

(a) He represents people in many cities in many countries?

(b) His name is unimportant: the story is about how appearances can be misleading?

(c) His name does not matter because the story is about the hypocrisy of society: we all tend to decide how important people are from their appearance?

(d) The author wishes to respect the young man's privacy: the removal of his clothes in hospital

165

(see page 66) deprives him of his life's props: he couldn't face losing them?

Add any other views you can think of.

9 Your impression of the young man from the first three paragraphs may be sharply altered by the information revealed in the final three paragraphs. What do you think the author wants us to learn from this experience?

10 Reread the fourth paragraph from the end of the story, beginning with 'Before his clothes were removed . . .' You will have noticed that the author writes the story as an observer. So that we can see things from the young man's point of view and know what he thinks and feels, reconstruct a portion of the story starting at a point which you think is suitable. You may write as the man if you wish, and stop at the point where his clothes begin to be removed in the hospital.

11 Society's attitudes to people based on their appearance seem to be very important in both this story and in 'The Blue Donkey' by Suniti Namjoshi (the two have been paired in this collection of stories). Write an essay in which you compare and contrast the two stories. (You will find it helpful to have decided on your interpretation of both stories before you begin.)

See also Activities 4, 6, 9 and 11 in the section 'Compare and Contrast Stories' on page 187.

The Blue Donkey

Before you start reading

1 It will be clear as you read this story that the blue donkey represents a particular group or groups of

people in society. As you read, try to make up your mind which group/groups the donkey represents, and whether such groups exist in our society.

During reading

2 The author's compact style of writing makes it useful to read the story carefully twice. During your second reading, work with a partner and jot down in two columns the arguments put by the two political parties in the first paragraph. Then decide together how rational you find their arguments.

After reading

3 Discuss your joint response to Activity 2 above with the rest of the class.

4 This story comes from a collection called 'The Blue Donkey Fables'. Fables are stories suggesting a moral or a 'message'. So that you and your partner(s) can decide what the author's intentions are, choose three or four statements from the following (add your own if you wish to), and place them in order of priority, with the one you support the most at the top:

(a) The story is about society's demands for conformity from those they consider different in some way.

(b) The story is about prejudice and the refusal to accept people for what they are.

(c) The story suggests that the problem lies with those who want the donkey to move away, not with the donkey.

(d) The story is about racism.

(e) The story is about the power of some who can harass the innocent and get away with it.

(f) The story is about the rejected minorities in all modern societies.

(g) The story shows how cleverly people will argue to cover up their prejudice and/or intolerance.

(h) The story is about kindness versus cruelty.

5 Now decide with your partner(s) your decision about Activity 1 above, and discuss it with other groups.

6 Each of us may construct a different meaning from this fable. Write an essay in which you argue the case for your interpretation. (You will find your answers to Activities 4 and 5 above useful in planning your essay.)

7 You may agree that this fable is written for adult readers – the author's language and economical style, among other things, suggest this. Reconstruct it so that it is suitable for young readers (you will need to decide which age group you wish to target your version for).

8 Write your own story in which a minority group (or person) is treated with discrimination.

9 You may have noticed that the author reveals little of what the blue donkey thinks and feels about its treatment. Rewrite this fable from the donkey's point of view, and if you wish to, use Suniti Namjoshi's compact style of writing.

See also Activities 4 and 9 in the section 'Compare and Contrast Stories' on page 187.

The Assignment

Before you start reading

1 You may have read stories or watched films that created great tension or suspense in you. In groups, try to recall examples and then discuss *how* the tension or suspense was generated. You may find the following a helpful start:

- by letting the character in the story/film face a situation which the reader/viewer knows is very dangerous, but about which the character is ignorant;
- by letting the reader/viewer emotionally share fully the danger that the character in the story/film faces and feels;
- by contrasting situations in which the reader/viewer feels relaxed and then very frightened;
- by a gradual or rapid build up of events which lead to a high risk climax.

Try to add to these possibilities from your own examples.

During reading

2 The power of this story lies partly in the suspense and tension it can generate in the reader.
   - Note, as you read, at what point *you* begin to feel the tension and/or suspense.
   - Try also to locate the place in the story where the author allows you to relax your tension.

This will help you to be aware of how the author controls your response to the story.

After reading

3 Which of the above techniques of creating tension/suspense does the author use in the story? Discuss with your partner(s) and make brief notes. Refer to evidence to support your views.

4 The last eight lines of the story have been printed separately on page 186.
   (a) Discuss with your partner(s) whether the ending of the story without these eight lines is satisfactory. If it isn't, how do you think the author ends his story, bearing in mind the development of events in it?

(b) If you *do* think the story seems complete without the last eight lines, what more may the author have in mind?

Now carefully predict in writing the author's ending. You may take up more than the eight lines the author does if you wish to. Try to use the author's direct and simple style. Your aim should be to make the ending as fitting to the story as you can. You may find it helpful to decide whether the story so far suggests a positive, a tragic or a surprise ending in some way.

5 Santokh Singh's role in this story needs careful consideration. Reread the last page of the story, beginning with '"Where is judge sahib?" he asked' and finishing with the author's own ending.

Does the author's portrayal make you and your partner:

(a) think well of Santokh?
(b) think very critically of him?
(c) feel that Santokh plays a neutral role?

Support your views with evidence. You may find the story's last line a significant starting point for forming your own views.

6 Notice that the author does not tell us what the armed men did. Was Manto right in leaving this description out? Discuss with your partner(s) and give reasons for your views.

7 Do you think the title is appropriate for the story? Give reasons for your answer.

8 Finally, try to decide about the author's intentions in writing this story. Which of these possibilities would you agree with? Manto wrote this story:

(a) to show his compassion for the innocent victims of violence;

(b) to show how people are prepared to kill in the name of religion;

(c) to show how sometimes the wrong decision can have fatal consequences;

(d) to show that what happens in this story can happen to other innocent people in other countries with different religions and races (for example, Jews and Arabs, Catholics and Protestants, white and black people).

Add other ideas of your own to this list.

9 Write an essay in which you:

(a) compare and contrast your ending (Activity 4) with the author's which you will find on page 186;

(b) argue the case as to which of these two endings is more fitting for the story.

10 Imagine you are directing a film based on this story. Pick a part of it that especially interests you and your partner(s) (for example, you could choose page 74 or the last page), and prepare:

(a) a story board – showing the settings in sequence, as well as the camera shots: which ones will be close-ups, which mid-length, and which long shots;

(b) the dialogue for each part of your sequence;

(c) the kind of music or sound effects you would want to use.

Finish with an explanation of how you went about Activities a, b and c above.

See also Activities 4, 6 and 11 in the section 'Compare and Contrast Stories' on page 187.

The Old Woman

Before you start reading

1 In small groups, discuss how far you agree or disagree
   with the following statements:
   (a) Grandparents have a low status in our society
       mainly because most of them are poor and no
       longer make a contribution to our society through
       work.
   (b) Grandparents have little or no status in families
       in our society: people prefer that they live apart
       on their own.
   (c) If grandparents lived with the families of their
       sons and daughters (ie in extended families),
       they may enjoy more care and respect.
   (d) Extended families are not always happy: there
       can be frictions between the members.

   Groups may wish to report back their views on the
   above issues.

During reading

2 As you read this story, try to decide on the status of
   the old woman in her family – is it better or worse
   than those of the elderly people you discussed above?

After reading

3 After a brief open discussion on Activity 2 above,
   work with your partner(s) and make notes on the
   following:
   (a) How does the author describe the old woman's
       status?
   (b) How far are her views and wishes taken seriously?
   (c) Why, after Nanda's death, was his family putting
       pressure on Menaka to leave?

4 With your partner(s), decide which of the following
   statements about the story you would agree with:

(a) The old woman may seem eccentric, but she is shrewd and knows what is going on around her.

(b) The old woman showed determination in hanging on after her husband died, and has established a special role for herself in the family.

(c) The old woman was right to advise Menaka about how to stay in the family: she once had to struggle to do the same herself.

(d) The story shows that status arises from the affection of the younger generation for the elderly.

(e) The story shows that the young have something to learn from the experience of the elderly.

(f) The story suggests that if Menaka had a job, she might have been treated differently.

Add other comments on the story that may have occurred to you.

5 Although the author has chosen to call this story 'The Old Woman', he could perhaps also have called it 'The Survivor'. Discuss and decide whether the author's choice is the better.

6 Make up the conversation between the old woman and Menaka as suggested in the final paragraph of the story.

7 Continue the story from where it stops. You will need to decide first whether it is the old woman who is your central character, or Menaka, or whether both occupy equal attention.

See also Activity 10 in the section 'Compare and Contrast Stories' on page 187.

The Shelter

Before you start reading

1 Quarrels may hurt but they may also have advantages. How do you think quarrels can be useful? Hold a class discussion.

2 Can the weather affect how we feel, or have some effect on our moods? How? Hold a class discussion.

During reading

3 As you read, try to be aware how the weather contributes to the story.

After reading

4 Except for the rain, the couple would not have met under the banyan tree. How else do you think the rain and the tree link with the story – with the couple's relationship? Discuss with your partner(s) and make brief notes.

5 With your partner(s) discuss whether you think the wife should have returned the night she left, or was it best that they went their separate ways? Argue both sides of the case and then offer your conclusion.

6 The author does not name his characters. How do you think this is significant? (With your partner(s) think of reasons why he may have chosen to leave out the names.)

7 After discussion with your partner(s), prepare in detail the friendship agreement prepared by the husband and wife. You may find the third paragraph of the story helpful.

8 Reread the fourth paragraph of 'The Shelter' and write a story about what happened to the wife that night as she walked out.

9 Near the end of the story, the husband says, 'I am changed now' and his wife replies, 'So am I.'

Imagine he locates her address and writes to her. Write this letter as well as her reply.

10 You may have noticed that the author is outside the story and tells it as an observer. Retell the story either from the woman's point of view (you may write as the woman), or from the man's point of view (you may write as the man).

11 Write a story with one of these titles:
    - 'A Chance Encounter'
    - 'An Unexpected Meeting'
    - 'The Reunion'
    - 'The End of Something'.

See also Activity 10 in the section 'Compare and Contrast Stories' on page 187.

Running Away from Home

Before you start reading

1 (a) With your partner(s), brainstorm ideas to fill out the following diagram, which is about the different situations from which people may run away:

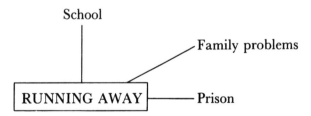

    (b) Gather the group's ideas on the blackboard for comment. Discuss any personal experiences of running away, or feeling like running away, from a situation.

During reading

2   You will notice that the author has avoided punctuation altogether – the whole story is a single sentence!

As you read, try to decide what effect Kamala Das achieves by the removal of punctuation:
- How does it physically affect your reading?
- Do you think the author wants us to experience some difficulty with making sense of what is going on? If so, why?

After reading

3 As a class, discuss your responses to Activity 2.

4 Kamala Das, as author, must have strong feelings about the characters she writes about in her story. With your partner list suitable words/phrases which show how *she* feels towards:
- Minnie
- Minnie's husband
- Minnie's father
- the lawyer at the end of the story.

(Is she, for example, critical, sympathetic, pitying, disapproving, angry, etc?)

5 With your partner(s) jot down reasons why Minnie leaves home. Do you think she was right to run away? Explain your views.

6 What emotions does the ending of the story make you and your partner(s) feel? Explain why.

7 The author must have had particular reasons for writing this story. Decide with your partner(s) how many of the following reflect these:
- (a) to show the tragic life of one woman;
- (b) to show that there are probably many Minnies in many male dominated societies;

(c) to show that Minnie is selfish and should not have run away;

(d) to show how awful some men can be;

(e) to show that Minnie could have survived independently if only she could find a job;

(f) to show that Minnie is like a bird trapped in a cage

(g) to express her anger.

Make up other statements you can think of.

8 What are your own impressions of Minnie? What impressions of womanhood do we have from the author's portrayal of Minnie? With your partner, discuss and make notes.

9 What are your own impressions of:
   – Minnie's husband?
   – Minnie's father?
   – the lawyer friend?

   What impressions of men do we have from the author's portrayal of these three men?

10 Continue the story from where it leaves off. (You may find it easier to punctuate your story!)

11 Rewrite the ending to the story. If you wish, you could write it to give the lawyer a more positive and supportive role.

12 Imagine and reconstruct Minnie's day *before* the day she decides to run away from home. Write this out as a (punctuated?) story.

See also Activity 10 in the section 'Compare and Contrast Stories' on page 187.

The Babus of Nayanjore

Before you start reading

Read the first four paragraphs of the story stopping

after 'an empty family chest', and then work with your
partner(s) to note brief responses to Activities 1 and 2.

1 The early introduction of contrasts in this story
   suggests that they may play an important role in it.
   From your reading of the story's opening, which of
   the following contrasts do you think the story is most
   likely to be about?

   (a) an extraordinary past versus an ordinary present;
   (b) social class: Kailas Babu versus the narrator;
   (c) character contrast: Kailas Babu versus the
       narrator;
   (d) our view of Kailas Babu versus the narrator's
       view of him;
   (e) dreams versus reality.

2 How we feel about Kailas Babu will be determined
   by *what* the narrator chooses to tell us, and *how* he
   chooses to do so. From your reading so far, is the
   narrator likely to be sympathetic to or critical of
   Kailas Babu? Refer to the text to support your views.

During reading

3 Pause after reading part 1 of the story (page 100),
   and reconsider your answer to Activity 2 above:

   (a) How has Kailas Babu been portrayed – sympa-
       thetically, critically, a mixture of the two or
       neutrally? Refer to the text to support your views.
   (b) Using single words or phrases, jot down some of
       the Babu's positive qualities as well as his weak-
       nesses from the story so far.
   (c) In the same way, jot down briefly what the
       narrator reveals about himself as a person (we
       learn more about him in section 2 of the story).

After reading

4 Skim read the first seven paragraphs of part 2, ending
   with 'because I was so good.' Do you and your

partner(s) think the narrator's self-praise here is serious, or is it a criticism of himself as he looks back on his earlier life? Explain your views.

5 The narrator's portrayal of his character in part 2 contrasts with Kailas Babu's in part 1. What difference(s) between the two men do you think the narrator intends us to notice? Discuss with your partner(s) and note down your views.

6 The narrator's deceitful practical joke on Kailas Babu (about which the narrator is very honest with the reader!) becomes a significant learning experience for him. How does he change in his attitude to
– Kusum, the Babu's grand-daughter?
– Kailas Babu?
– himself?
Discuss with your partner(s) and make notes.

7 Kailas Babu may have lost his wealth but not the dignity and pride of his family's history: they are all he has. By contrast, the narrator's family history was very humble, but he felt he had raised his status through his education. Reread Activity 1 and decide finally with your parner(s) which of the five options suggested there best sum up what the story is about. (Add other possibilities that may occur to you.)

8 Whereas Kailas Babu remains consistently himself, the narrator's character changes by the end of the story. How far do you agree with this view of the story? Write an essay giving your reasons for agreeing or disagreeing with this view.

9 More than anything else, the story is about social class and how this influences the development of a person's character and values. Write an essay in which you argue the case for or against this view of the story.

See also Activity 4 in the section 'Compare and Contrast Stories' on page 187.

Charity

Before you start reading

1 In small groups, discuss how far you agree or disagree with these statements:

   (a) Charities exist because governments do little to end ugly inequalities in our society (and in many others).

   (b) As long as charities remain, ugly inequalities will also remain.

   (c) The well-off contribute occasionally to charity to ease their conscience; their giving involves no personal sacrifice.

   (d) Well-off countries, like well-off people, are powerful; poor countries, like poor people, are powerless.

   (e) Power and inequality are linked.

2 You may wish to come together to report back your views on the above issues.

During reading

3 Pause after reading part 2 of the story. With your partner(s), tackle the following:

   (a) Construct a quick simple sketch to show the layout of the enclosures and the gates.

   (b) What do you make of Majumdar's plan – will it work?

   (c) What would you predict will happen when the one and only entrance gate is opened to let the public in?

   (d) How genuine do you think Majumdar's intentions are?

After reading

4 Reconsider your responses to Activities 3b, c and d above: how far did the rest of the story confirm your predictions?

   Discuss with your partner(s) and make brief notes.

5 Part 3 of the story describes the response of the public in the days leading up to the day of charity. Working with your partner:

   (a) Reread the first paragraph of this part to establish the range of people who come to Majumdar's charity day.

   (b) Reread the second paragraph to decide what all the fatal accidents reveal about people.

6 In the final three paragraphs of part 3, the author comments on the crowds waiting to enter the enclosures. Pick two or three short quotations (a sentence or two each) that show the author's viewpoint. Do you and your partner(s) agree with his viewpoint?

7 From the first seven paragraphs of part 4 ending with 'let yourself go with the crowd', choose a few short quotations that show how money affects the behaviour of different people. Work with your partner(s).

8 Decide which of the statements below best represent the author's intentions in writing this story. (You may find it helpful to decide whether the emphasis is on Majumdar and his charity, or on how money affects people's attitudes, or indeed on both.)

   (a) The ending of the story shows how Mymoon Bibi, a poor woman, was worse off at the end of Majumdar's charity than at the beginning.

   (b) Mymoon Bibi's fate represents the fate of all the poor in this story.

   (c) The story is about the hypocrisy of the charitable: Majumdar will eventually gain more from his charity than he has lost.

(d) The story shows that power and equality are linked.

(e) The story is really about the greed and selfishness of people in most societies.

(f) The story shows one against all and all against one in the pursuit of money.

(g) The story shows how people can treat others to move ahead in a competitive society.

Add any other views you may have.

9 Pick one statement (or two?) that you think most represents what the story is about from the choice given for Activity 8 above. Using this as your starting point, write an essay to argue your interpretation of the story.

10 Imagine you could interview Majumdar on the radio about what he did, his intentions, the outcomes of his charity and the future. Write out your interview in the form of a playscript. (You will need to decided how shrewd Majumdar is, your own attitude to him as a journalist, what your programme listeners will want to know, and how closely you will want to interview him.)

11 Imagine Mymoon Bibi writes a letter about her experiences either to Majumdar or to a newspaper. Write out this letter.

See also Activity 4 in the section 'Compare and Contrast Stories' on page 187.

And Now She's Dead

Before you start reading
1 How true do you and your partner(s) think these

statements are:

(a) Some people are forced to keep up a pretence of one kind or another to cope with life.

(b) Some people choose to keep up a pretence of one kind or another to cope with life.

Jot down specific examples in which (a) and/or (b) are true (eg. at work, in social situations, parents in relation to children)

During reading

2 Pause after reading up to 'I was to start working from the next day' (page 125) to consider these two questions:

(a) What role does the narrator play in this story?

(b) How does the narrator's attitude affect our attitude, as readers, to Kartar Singh?

After reading

3 'You speak the truth, Janab. Now she is really dead.' (page 136) How many 'deaths' does 'the truth' actually bring about?

Discuss this with your partner(s) and make notes.

4 To help Kartar Singh, the narrator advises him: 'Tell the Mem Sahib that your wife died in child birth.' How wise is this advice, bearing in mind the effect it has on Kartar Singh? Discuss with your partner and make notes.

5 Reconsider the statements 1(a) and (b) above. Which of them applies to Kartar Singh? Give reasons for your views.

6 Which of these statements do you and your partner(s) agree with?

(a) The story suggests that pretence helps people to cope with life.

(b) The story suggests that no matter how painful the truth is, it is better to live with it.

(c) The story is not really about marriage but about the human desire and need for companionship.

(d) The story is about a very unlucky person.

(e) Kartar Singh's problems are probably faced by some people in our society.

(f) Kartar Singh was a victim of a sexist attitude on the part of his employer.

Add other statements you can think of.

7 Imagine, as the story ends, that Kartar Singh decides to tell the truth to his employer, the head Mem Sa'ab. Reread pages 135–6 and then write out in story or play-form his conversation with her.

See also Activities 3, 8 and 13 in the section 'Compare and Contrast Stories' on page 187.

A Dead Wife

Before you start reading

1 What are the various reasons for which people – of whatever culture – get married? Brainstorm ideas on the blackboard.

During reading

2 Read the first three paragraphs of the story as a whole class and decide: who is the narrator and what do we know about her?

After reading

3 Reread the first paragraph of the story and the paragraph on page 140 beginning, 'I was worried, too . . .'. What do these paragraphs reveal about the narrator and her attitude to Mr Varma? Discuss with your partner(s) and make notes.

4 Jot down reasons why you and your partner(s) think:

(a) Mr Varma chose to remarry so soon after his first wife died.

(b) The second Mrs Varma agreed to marry her husband.

(c) The narrator's mother is sympathetic to Mrs Varma.

(d) The narrator is critical of Mr Varma's second marriage.

5 Whose point of view do you support – the narrator's or her mother's? Discuss with your partner(s) and explain your choice.

6 With your partner consider carefully the title in relation to the story. Whom does it refer to – the first wife or the second – or both?

7 Reread pages 143–4. Judging by the last three paragraphs, how do you think the narrator feels towards Mrs Varma? Discuss with your partner and make notes.

8 The servant in the narrator's house, Jugni, says, 'The new bride really belongs to the lower class.' Look for evidence to support this view.

Now discuss these two statements with your partner(s) and decide which you agree with:

(a) The story is about an unsatisfactory marriage.

(b) The story is about social class and exploitation.

Add other statements if you wish to.

9 Continue writing the story from where it leaves off.

10 Imagine that the narrator goes to meet the new Mrs Varma. Describe what happens.

11 Retell the story from Mrs Varma's point of view.

See also Activities 5, 11 and 13 in the section 'Compare and Contrast Stories' on page 187.

'The Assignment' by Sadaat H Manto

Here are the last eight lines of the story which were omitted from page 76:

As Santokh Singh turned the corner, four men, their faces covered with their turbans, moved towards him. Two of them held burning oil torches, the others carried cans of kerosene oil and explosives. One of them asked Santokh, 'Sardar Ji, have you completed your assignment?'

The young man nodded.

'Should we then proceed with ours?' he asked.

'If you like,' he replied and walked away.

Compare and Contrast Stories

1 'A Devoted Son' by Anita Desai and 'Smoke' by Ila Mehta focus on the theme of duty. Write an essay based on these stories in which you explore this theme. You may like to finish by indicating what conclusions you draw from your study.

2 Both 'A Devoted Son' by Anita Desai and 'Smoke' by Ila Mehta are concerned with family relationships. Compare and contrast Rakesh's role as a son and Shubha's role as a daughter-in-law in their respective families.

3 'Smoke' by Ila Mehta and 'And Now She's Dead' by G Broker were both translated from the Gujarati. Write an essay in which you explore how successfully a translated story can convey the thoughts, feelings, attitudes and social situation(s) of another culture.

   You may find the following suggestions helpful in preparing your essay:
   - Is it possible to tell whether these stories are in translation? If so, what evidence can you find?
   - Are there passages where you cannot tell whether the stories are translated? If so, choose two (or more) short extracts of what you consider Standard English, one from each story, and comment on
     (a) how you find the language convincing, ie. suited to the author's purposes/intentions and
     (b) how the language strikes you as a reader.

- Examine the dialogue in the two stories: what comments would you want to make on the language used?
- Examine pieces of description from each story: how convincing is the choice of language used?
- Are there ways in which the language used reveals things recognisably Indian? Can you give examples?
- Is one of the two stories more successful than the other as a translation, or do you find both have equal merit?

4 Although all these stories are South Asian, many of them deal with issues that affect us all, whatever our nationality or culture (for example, 'The Blue Donkey', 'Overcoat', 'The Assignment', 'The Babus of Nayanjore' and 'Charity'). Choose two or three stories that particularly appealed to you and discuss how they are universal in their concern.

5 Although most of the stories in this collection are written originally in English, they are recognisably Indian in many ways (for example, 'The Bhorwani Marriage' and 'A Dead Wife'). Choose two or three that you enjoyed reading and discuss this issue. Think about:
- the settings and their contribution;
- the characters: their treatment of each other, their language, values, attitudes, habits etc;
- style: the author's choice of language and the occasional use of Indian expressions;
- attitudes to particular issues such as family loyalties and duties, marriage, religion, behaviour with the opposite sex etc.

Include other aspects that strike you as relevant for comment

6 The endings of some of these stories are especially

significant (for example, 'The Bride', 'Overcoat', 'The Assignment'). Basing your essay on two or three stories of your own choice, discuss how appropriate and significant you found the endings in relation to the stories.

(You may find it useful to begin by asking: what would each story lose if its ending were removed? This will help you to judge what contribution the ending makes to the whole story.)

7 Examine carefully the openings of two stories you liked. Explain how effective you found these openings, and how they related to the rest of the stories.

8 Marriage can make or break people's lives. Discuss the importance of marriage in 'Too Late for Anger', and 'And Now She's Dead'.

Can marriage make or break people's lives in our society in the same way? Comment on this to conclude your essay.

9 Stories in this collection have been placed alongside others to which they are related in some way. Your reading of the stories may have made you feel that they could have been grouped differently from the combination shown in the Contents list (for example, 'Overcoat', 'The Blue Donkey' and 'The Assignment'). Choose two stories from the Contents list and argue the case for or against their placement alongside each other.

10 Choose one of the following three essay titles which are all based on these stories:
   'The Old Woman' by M Bandyopadhyay
   'The Shelter' by R K Narayan
   'Running Away from Home' by K Das
   (a) What pictures of womanhood emerge from these stories? Could these women be from any

modern society, or do you think they belong to a particular cultural background? Explain your views.

(b) Compare and contrast the portrayal of women and men in the above stories. You may like to finish by indicating what conclusions you draw from your study.

(c) Imagine that the three central women characters in the three stories come together to discuss their different experiences of life. Write about their meeting in story or play form.

11 The titles of stories can have a special relationship with the stories (for example, 'A Devoted Son', 'Too Late for Anger', 'Overcoat', 'The Assignment' and 'A Dead Wife').

Choose two or three stories and explore
(a) what each title suggests on its own;
(b) how each title relates to the story;
(c) how appropriate you find it (and alternatives that may be/may not be suitable);
(d) whether or not the title can be interpreted in more than one way, and how this arises from your reading of the story;
(e) whether or not the author's intentions in writing the story are indicated by the title.

Add any other points you can think of to this list.

12 Several stories included in this anthology focus on the conflict between traditional and modern values (for example, 'Too Late for Anger', 'The First Party'). Write an essay in which you explore this conflict, discuss its consequences and comment on what you discover.

13 'And Now She's Dead' is written by a male author with a male narrator. By contrast, 'A Dead Wife' is written by a female author with a woman as

narrator. The first encourages our sympathy for a man as central character, while the second does so for a female central character. Compare and contrast the two stories in detail so that you can finish with a conclusion showing what you learned from your study.

Notes on Authors and Further Reading

The stories included in this book come from anthologies identified below.

Anita Desai (1931–   ) has established a high reputation as a writer of fiction. Her father was Bengali and her mother German. She was educated in Delhi. 'A Devoted Son' comes from her anthology called *Games at Twilight* (Penguin, 1982). Among her novels are the following:

Clear Light of Day (Penguin, 1980)

Fire on the Mountain (Penguin, 1981). (This book won two prestigious awards.)

The Village by the Sea (Penguin, 1982)

In Custody (Heinemann, 1984).

Ila Arab Mehta (1938–   ) is Professor of Gujarati at St Xaviers College, Bombay. She is an award-winning writer of short stories, plays and novels. She has also written for radio and television. 'Smoke' comes from *Truth Tales: Stories by Indian Women* (The Women's Press, 1986).

Murli Das Melwani (1939–   ) did an MA in English at Gauhati University. He teaches at Sankardar College, Shillong. 'The Bhorwani Marriage' comes from *Contemporary Indian-English Short Stories* edited by Madhusudan Prasad (Sterling, Delhi, 1983). Among his published works are the following:

Stories of a Salesman
Deep Roots, a three-act play
Themes in Indo-English Literature, a book of criticism.
(All published in India.)

Suniti Namjoshi (1941–) is a poet, satirist and fabulist, and has published her work in India, Canada, the USA and Britain. Since 1972, she has taught in the Department of English at the University of Toronto, and has recently spent time living and working in Devon. 'The Bride' and 'The Blue Donkey' come from *The Blue Donkey Fables*, (The Women's Press, 1988). Among her other publications are these titles:
Feminist Fables (Sheba, 1981)
The Conversations of a Cow (The Women's Press, 1985)
Aditi and the One-eyed Monkey, a children's book (Sheba, 1986)
Flesh and Paper with G Hanscombe (Ragweed, Canada, 1986).

Padma Perera was educated in India and at the University of Michigan, Ann Arbor. She has won several fellowships for her writing and teaches at the University of Colorado, Boulder. She has been an Indian dancer of the classical Manipuri style. 'Too Late for Anger' comes from *Birthday Deathday and other Stories* (The Women's Press, 1985). Her other published works include the following (published in India and the USA):
Coigns of Vantage (short stories), 1978
The Challenge of Indian Fiction in English, non-fiction.

Attia Hosain (1913–) was educated in India, and was the first woman to graduate from among the feudal 'Taluqdari' families into which she was born. She became a journalist, broadcaster and writer of fiction. After coming to England in 1947, she did her own programme on the BBC's Eastern Service, and has also appeared on television and the West End stage. 'The First Party' comes from the collection *Phoenix Fled* (Virago, 1988). Her novel *Sunlight on a Broken Column* was published by Heinemann, Delhi, 1981.

Ghulam Abbas (1909–1983) was educated at Lahore, Pakistan, and began writing in 1924. He worked as a producer for the BBC for four years, and was editor of a number of journals in Pakistan. He retired in 1967. His short story collection *Anandi* won a cash award from the Pakistan Government. The story included here, 'Overcoat', comes from *Selected Short Stories from Pakistan: Urdu*, edited by Ahmed Ali (Pakistan Academy of Letters, 1983).

Saadat Hasan Manto (1912–1955) worked as a journalist, screenwriter and broadcaster. He wrote many essays and plays, but it is above all on the over 200 short stories he wrote that his high reputation rests. Khalid Hasan, who translated some of Manto's stories from Urdu into English, says that Manto 'remains one of the world's major short story writers.' 'The Assignment' comes from *Kingdom's End and other Stories* translated by Khalid Hasan (Verso, 1987). This anthology is readily available in Britain.

Manik Bandyopadhyay (1908–1956) studied mathematics and science at University and during 26-year writing career, became one of Bengal's most important and prolific writers. His output includes 39 novels, 16 collections of short stories and over 200 other short stories printed in various periodicals. 'The Old Woman' comes from *Of Women, Outcastes, Peasants and Rebels: A Selection of Bengali Short Stories* edited, translated and with an introduction by Kalpana Bardhan (University of California Press, 1990).

R K Narayan (1907–) has long been recognised as one of India's most distinguished writers. Narayan, Mulk Raj Anand and Raj Rao are a trio that pioneered modern Indo-English fiction. He has published over 25 works, mostly novels, and has received several honours from literary societies, colleges and universities abroad. 'The Shelter' comes from *Contemporary Indian-English Stories* edited by Madhusudan Prasad (Sterling, New Delhi, 1983). Among his novels readily obtained in Britain are the following:
The Painter of Signs (Penguin, 1982)
The Vendor of Sweets (Penguin, 1983)
The Guide (Bodley Head, 1970)
Swami and Friends (OUP, 1978).

Kamala Das (1934–) is an Indo-English poet with a distinguished reputation as a writer of short stories. She is known for her frank and bold treatment of life in her works, and her autobiography, *My Life*, created quite a stir. Her *Collected Poems* in English won her the National Prize of the India Literary Academy in 1985, India's highest literary honour. 'Running Away from Home' comes from *Panorama: An Anthology of Modern Indian Short Stories* edited by M K Anand and S Balurao (Oriental University Press, 1987). This anthology is readily available in Britain.

Rabindranath Tagore (1861–1941) was during his lifetime, regarded as the greatest writer from South Asia, and his reputation today remains very high. His creative gifts shone in poetry, prose, music and painting. He was awarded the Nobel Prize for Literature in 1913 mainly for his poems, translated in the anthology called 'Gitanjali'. He wrote about a hundred short stories. 'The Babus of Nayanjore' comes from the collection called *Hungry Stones* translated from Bengali into English by several authors (Macmillan, India, 1985). One of Tagore's novels, *The Home and the World* is published by Penguin (1985).

Shaukat Osman (1917–   ) is a major novelist, short story writer and playwright from Bangladesh. He is also highly regarded as an essayist and as an author of children's literature. Osman did an MA in Bengali language and literature at the University of Calcutta, and was awarded the Bengali Academy prize for his short stories in 1962. 'Charity' comes from *Selected Stories: Shaukat Osman*, introduced and translated by Osman Jamal (Bangla Academy, Dhaka, 1985).

Gulabhdas Broker (1909–   ) is a graduate of the University of Bombay. He is highly regarded for his short stories and one-act plays (written in Gujarati), and has published eleven short story collections. A number of his stories have been translated into other Indian as well as European languages. 'And Now She's Dead' was published in *Panorama – An Anthology of Modern Indian Short Stories* edited by Mulk Raj Anand and S Balurao (Oriental University Press, 1987). This anthology is readily available in Britain.

Sunita Jain obtained a PhD from the University of Nebraska, and teaches English. She writes fiction as well as poetry both in English and Hindi, and has published novels, collections of short stories and poems abroad. Her work in English has won her several literary awards in the USA. 'A Dead Wife' comes from *Contemporary Indian-English Stories* edited by Madhusudan Prasad (Sterling, New Delhi, 1983).

NB.   In addition to the above anthologies the reader may find the following titles of interest:

The Inner Courtyard – Stories by Indian Women edited by Laxmi Holmstrom (Virago, 1990).

Stories from South Asia edited by John Welch (OUP, 1988).

Right of Way – prose and poetry by the Asian Women Writers' workshop (The Women's Press, 1988).

Short Stories from India, Pakistan and Bangladesh edited by Ranjana Ash (Harrap, 1980).

The Middle Man and other Stories by Bharati Mukherji (Virago, 1989).

Malgudi Days by R K Narayan (King Penguin, 1984).

Rabindranath Tagore – Selected Short Stories, translated and introduced by William Radice (Penguin 1991).

The following anthologies by Farukh Dhondy:
East End at Your Feet (Macmillan Topliner, 1986).
Come to Mecca (Fontana, 1978).
Trip Trap (Armada Lions, 1984).

'ATCAL READING GUIDES – African, Caribbean and Indo-British Literature for the Classroom' ed. by John Stephens (ATCAL Publications and The English Centre, 1988).
This is an extremely useful annotated reading guide for teachers, and the contributors' experience as teachers shows in their comments on each book. It is available from The English and Media Centre, Sutherland Street, London, SW1V 4LH.

Book Title: STORIES FROM ASIA

New Longman Literature
Post-1914 Fiction

Susan Hill	*I'm the King of the Castle* 0 582 22173 0
	The Woman in Black 0 582 02660 1
	The Mist in the Mirror 0 582 25399 3
Aldous Huxley	*Brave New World* 0 582 06016 8
Robin Jenks	*The Cone-Gatherers* 0 582 06017 6
Doris Lessing	*The Fifth Child* 0 582 06021 4
Joan Lindsay	*Picnic at Hanging Rock* 0 582 08174 2
Bernard MacLaverty	*Lamb* 0 582 06557 7
Brian Moore	*Lies of Silence* 0 582 08170 X
George Orwell	*Animal Farm* 0 582 06010 9
F Scott Fitzgerald	*The Great Gatsby* 0 582 06023 0
Robert Swindells	*Daz 4 Zoe* 0 582 30243 9
Anne Tyler	*A Slipping-Down Life* 0 582 29247 6
Virginia Woolf	*To the Lighthouse* 0 582 09714 2

Post-1914 Short Stories

Angelou, Goodison, Senior & Walker	*Quartet of Stories* 0 582 28730 8
Stan Barstow	*The Human Element and Other Stories* 0 582 23369 0
Roald Dahl	*A Roald Dahl Selection* 0 582 22281 8
selected by Geoff Barton	*Stories Old and New* 0 582 28931 9
selected by Madhu Bhinda	*Stories from Africa* 0 582 25393 4
	Stories from Asia 0 582 03922 3
selected by Celeste Flower	*Mystery and Horror* 0 582 28928 9
selected by Jane Christopher	*War Stories* 0 582 28927 0
selected by Susan Hill	*Ghost Stories* 0 582 02661 X
selected by Beverley Naidoo, Christine Donovan & Alun Hicks	*Global Tales* 0 582 28929 7
selected by Andrew Whittle & Roy Blatchford	*Ten D H Lawrence Short Stories* 0 582 29249 2

Post-1914 Poetry

collected & edited by Roy Blatchford	*Voices of the Great War* 0 582 29248 4
edited by George MacBeth	*Poetry 1900-1975* 0 582 35149 9
edited by Julia Markus & Paul Jordan	*Poems 2* 0 582 25401 9

Post-1914 Plays

Alan Ayckbourn	*Absent Friends* 0 582 30242 0
Terrence Rattigan	*The Winslow Boy* 0 582 06019 2
Jack Rosenthal	*P'Tang, Yang, Kipperbang and other TV Plays* 0 582 22389 X
Willy Russell	*Educating Rita* 0 582 06013 3
	Shirley Valentine 0 582 08173 4
selected by Geoff Barton	*Ten Short Plays* 0 582 25383 7
selected by Michael Marland	*Scenes from Plays* 0 582 25394 2
Peter Shaffer	*The Royal Hunt of the Sun* 0 582 06014 1
	Equus 0 582 09712 6
Bernard Shaw	*Pygmalion* 0 582 06015 X
	Saint Joan 0 582 07786 9
Sheridan, Richard Brinsley	*The Rivals/The School for Scandal* 0 582 25396 9

Acknowledgements

We are grateful to the following for permission to reproduce stories:

Bangla Academy for 'Charity' by Shaukat Osman in *Selected Short Stories: Shaukat Osman* (1985); William Heinemann Ltd for 'A Devoted Son' in *Games at Twilight* by Anita Desai; Kali for Women and The Women's Press Ltd for 'Smoke' by Ila Arab Mehta in *Truth Tales: Stories by Indian Women* (first published in English by Kali for Women 1986/The Women's Press Ltd 1986); Macmillan, London and Basingstoke, for 'The Babus of Nayanjore' in *Hungry Stones* by Rabindranath Tagore (1985); Sterling Publishers Pvt Ltd for 'A Dead Wife' by Sunita Jain, 'The Bhorwani Marriage' by Murli Das Melwani and 'The Shelter' by R K Narayan in Contemporary Indian-English Stories edited by Madhusudan Prasad (1983), and 'And Now She's Dead' by Gulabdas Broker and 'Running Away from Home' by Kamala Das in *Panorama: An Anthology of Modern Indian Short Stories* (1987); University of California Press for 'The Old Woman' by Manik Bandyopadhyay in *Of Women, Outcastes, Peasants and Rebels: A Selection of Bengali Short Stories* edited, translated and with an introduction by Kalpana Bardhan (1990), copyright (c) 1990 The Regents of the University of California; Verso Ltd for 'The Assignment' in *Kingdom's End and Other Stories* by Saadat Hasan Manto (1987); Virago Press Ltd for 'The First Party' in *Phoenix Fled* by Attia Hosain (1988); The Women's Press Ltd for 'The Bride' and 'The Blue Donkey' in *The Blue Donkey Fables* by Suniti Namjoshi (1988), and 'Too Late for Anger' by Padma Perera in *Birthday Deathday and Other Stories* (1985)

We have been unable to trace the copyright holder in 'The Overcoat' by Ghulam Abbas in *Selected Stories from Pakistan Urdu* edited by Ahmed Ali (Pakistan Academy of Letters, 1983) and would appreciate any information that would enable us to do so.

Cover: Peter Sanders
Cover design by Ship

Pearson Education Limited
Edinburgh Gate, Harlow, Essex CM20 2JE, England
and Associated Companies throughout the world.

© Longman Group UK Limited 1992

First published 1992
Sixteenth impression 2008

ISBN 978-0-582-03922-3

Set in 11/13 point Baskerville, Linotron 202
Printed in Malaysia, PA